L...
of the
Goddess

Lamp
of the
Goddess

Lives and
Teachings of a
Priestess

Rae Beth

SAMUEL WEISER, INC.

York Beach, Maine

First published in the United States in 1995 by
Samuel Weiser, Inc.
P. O. Box 612
York Beach, ME 03910-0612

04 03 02 01 00 99 98 97 96 95
10 09 08 07 06 05 04 03 02 01

Library of Congress Cataloging-in-Publication Data
Beth, Rae.
     [Reincarnation and the dark goddess]
     Lamp of the goddess : lives and teachings of a
priestess / Rae Beth.
        p. cm.
Originally published: Reincarnation and the dark god
dess.   London :   Robert Hale.
     Includes Bibliographical references.
     ISBN 0-87728-848-8
     1. Beth, Rae.   2. Fellowhip of Isis--Biography.
3. Women priests--England--Biography.
4. Goddess religion.   5. Paganism.
I. Title.
BP605.F44B48   1995
299'.93--dc20   95-16719
MG   CIP

Cover illustration by Barbara Walton. Used by permission of
Robert Hale, Ltd.

Printed in the United States of America

• Contents •

As it was,
As it is,
As it shall be
Evermore,
O Thou Triune
Of Grace!
With the ebb,
With the flow,
O Thou Triune
Of Grace!
With the ebb,
With the flow.

Anon

(collected by Alexander Carmichael)

Introduction

One of the tragedies of the age which is now drawing to a close has been the loss to communities in Europe and the West of all those who had the temperament and skill for the priesthood, but were disqualified in some way by the Church. For a start, no priestesses were permitted to work, since all women were ruled out by reason of their supposed spiritual and intellectual inferiority. Some men, also, have been excluded, either for social or political reasons, or because of their non-Christian or heretical beliefs. But now, there are signs that this situation is changing. A new Goddess-worshipping tradition is establishing itself, a new Pagan faith, alongside and even blended with a new expression of other faiths, including (in some circles) a redefined Christianity. People are having new thoughts about what makes a priestly or priestessly life, and deciding it has to do with mediation of the Spirit (however we choose to name this) and not always with tradition and formality. It is also about counselling and advising, or facilitating, when people are going through rites of passage, like birth, puberty, marriage, spiritual initiation or death. This is based in celebration of the cycles of nature, in respect of their subtle and psychic effect upon us, as well as in terms of the old agricultural year. But it is not about laying down the law nor assuming a moral superiority over people whose beliefs or experiences differ from our own. Instead, it is unassuming and gentle and exploratory.

From this, it will be seen that many are already doing the work, who perhaps would not lay claim to the title. And there are many more who could be doing it and, as they may sense, have often done so in past incarnations. This book is for them, the priestesses who are unknown (and the priests, too) because it is about my own past lives and present day knowledge. None of it is vindicated or affirmed by the culture that we live in (yet) but is nevertheless of interest, I hope, and a potential encouragement to others on the same path.

This book is also for all those who acknowledge the new priestesses, and 'alternative' priests, without necessarily wanting to be amongst them. For in rethinking what we mean by or expect of the priesthood, we can free our own spiritual selves to choose our direction.

Since it is my belief that, to do this work, we must first reclaim words like 'spirit' and 'holy' and 'psychic' from the land of hypocrisy and cliché, and because my own ministry concerns word-magic and the mysteries of divination and prophecy, and because of my ordination, I have here written about the Dark Goddess of Spirit Realms, rather than about Mother Goddess as nature's wisdom, in the concrete and physical sense. This is a dimension where personal experience counts for everything - or should, if we are not to establish another kind of dogma! It has been, in its unconventional manifestations, relegated to the 'lunatic fringe' of mediums and fortune tellers - seen like that and despised for it! But what treasure is hidden in the world of our *individual* psychic experiences and inner senses? These are things that most people don't usually talk about, yet they are sacred and can contain deep knowledge. If we all started to share our experiences with each other, not to try and impress or pull 'spiritual rank', but humanly and sympathetically, the world might begin to change. At the very least, our collective feeling about 'the meaning in it all' could become enhanced. But first, we need to uncover our buried knowledge that the Deep Feminine is not a realm or a quality of dubious morality nor of superstition. We need to reapproach the Dark Goddess, knowing She's the Presence of the Otherworld and spirit communications and all visionary and psychic experience and neither fearing Her nor misunderstanding Her. I offer this book as a contribution to the sharing of inwardness, by which we can help each other along this exciting and challenging path.

Blessed Be

Rae Beth
Summer Solstice - 1993
Bath

1

The Great Matrix

The feminine has been defined as the personal and associated with an undue attachment to personal experience,
one's own history. That which is feminine has been
aligned with subjectivity and an intuitive manner of relating to
life, then consigned to the rubbish heap, labelled 'trivia and
superstition' by the dominant culture and therefore by patriarchy. This has been the way of things for many thousand
years. But life is beginning to change, everywhere. There is a
tremendous growth of modern Goddess spirituality, for both
women and men (in the West, anyway, where it has been most
suppressed) and an upsurge of feminist consciousness throughout the world. We still have a long way to go. But the signs are
all there that the day when men and women can stand equal in
friendship, and when the Mother of all Life and the All-Father
can be honoured equally as deities, could dawn now.

The impetus for this change is coming from the Feminine -
from the return to the Goddess as divinity within all, in all created things and in Earth Herself - as much as from feminist
political consciousness. And it is true that this is personal. An
early feminist catchphrase was 'the personal is political'. In the
realm of Goddess spirituality, the personal is also spiritual, or
rather the spiritual is experienced personally. This brings all
our spirituality right back home into our innermost selves, at
the core of our being on Earth with each other. A living and
felt essence, beyond dogma, and ours to nurture and develop

and also to commune from with others and with whom or whatsoever we worship. Autonomous and true and subject to no-one's authority but our own inner sense of what is true and right. All this is a very long way from established Church teachings, as these have formed present-day Western culture and still inform it, and it is also as far as you can get from patriarchal attitudes.

It is our hope for the future, because personal responsibility for the effect of our lives on Earth cannot be quite complete when personal experience is neither owned nor valued in that most personal area of our lives - individual psychic knowing and beliefs about spirit. Therefore, I wish to tell about my own experiences of the Deep Feminine aspect of 'Creator Spirit', as inwardness. Not the Earth Mother, but the Dark Goddess of the Spirit Realm, She who presides over psychic dimensions of Birth, Death and Sex and rules the dream world. Goddess of all that affects us most powerfully in our own souls. I want to tell it all in terms of my own spiritual autobiography as Her priestess. Though what I mean by that word is not a feminine and Pagan equivalent of a Christian priest but something much closer to a Pagan medium, a mediator of the spirit, and not therefore an annexer of spiritual authority from other worshippers. What follows will be a thoroughly personal account. The point of it is to contribute to the reowning and reaffirming of all individual spiritual perceptions of the Deep Feminine, and to encourage other people in their own valuing of their deep spiritual insights, as well as quite simply to share what I have learned.

The Deep Feminine - or Dark Goddess - was worshipped by Pagans of old as She still is now, by many modern Pagans, here in what is called 'the civilized world'. She is also worshipped in the East, by Hindus, Tibetan Buddhists and others. Kali, Tara, Isis, the Shekinah, Anu, Mari, Morgaine, Persephone. These are some of Her names from around the world. Erishkegal, Hecate, Morrighan, Sulis, Rhiannon, Lilith, Black Madonna and Mary Magdalene. These last two are the names by which She has been known to heretical Christians. The Dark Goddess has never been absent from the world, though Her worship has been suppressed. (And even in the Eastern religions where She has been acknowledged, Her importance and power have been both distorted and understated.)

She may be best known to those who have had no name for Her, but who value subjective experience - in balance with the objective approach to obtainable facts - and understand direct revelation as rightly accessible to each one of us. I am thinking of many artists and psychic investigators and visionaries.

There is, nowadays, a serious lack of vital imaginative feeling. That is because, for a very long time, we have been taught by Church and State to mistrust our intuitions or fear them as heresy. Direct revelation or personal ideas about the mysterious side of life were, quite rightly, perceived as subversive, because they could end up challenging the prevailing system of values and spiritual ethos of established society. Those who persisted were imprisoned and tortured, hanged, burned or shot. Yet without intuitions and consciousness of a real personal relationship with spirit presences, as well as the chance to decide for oneself about the great spiritual questions of life, there is deadlock in the soul. We have lost the true meaning of life as a quest for transformation into other spheres than the mundane, for transcendence to poetry, ecstasy, beauty, communion with each other on the deepest level and a sense of wonder. Many people fill this emptiness with television and a concentration on plans for a holiday or social events, yet still wander through life in a haze of uncertainty and frustration, with underlying angst, as a look at the faces passing on any street will soon make clear. (It is not even conscious pain that most people feel - yet pain at least lets us know how much we are alive!) Since intuition and psychic meaning, an inner richness and profound sense of challenge, have been traditionally associated with the Dark Goddess, and since our culture has long refused to honour Her, this is hardly surprising.

The story that I am going to tell concerns men as well as women. Men, too, have psychic knowing, intuitions, revelations, visions that may be at variance with all orthodox teachings. The touch of the Dark Goddess is also felt within masculine consciousness, though obviously men do not identify with a mediation of the Deep Feminine in the same way that a woman can. In a parallel fashion the vital truth of the God, the Masculine aspect of 'Creator Spirit', is as accessible to women as men, though they do not experience a mediation of Him in the same way that men do. These things are bound up with concepts of masculine and feminine and yet are beyond gender. This is because the Dark Goddess is not a 'spirit woman' on a grand scale. She is actually a spiritual power, manifesting in a variety of ways. (Similarly, the God, the Father of Life, is not a huge man in the sky, not in anyone's religion! Nor a huge man in the Inner Realm. He is, however, much we have misunderstood Him, a spiritual power of a certain kind, both immanent and transcendent.) In spite of the fact that spirit guides with a human visual aspect, or the appearance of one, can mediate to us the Presence of either a Goddess or God, anthropomorphism breaks down at a certain point, as does our human concept of gender and sexuality. Women do manifestly mediate the Goddess and it has been truly said that every woman is Isis. And yet to speak of the Goddess as a human female on a cosmic scale is to miss the point that She is more than human - and also is more than female as we understand the word.

But now, who am I to tell you my own story? And why on Earth is it you'd want to know? First and foremost I'm a fellow human being with a story to tell. (More dramatic than a soap opera, I promise you!) Secondly, I am a practising witch, right now in the twentieth century. By this I mean a person who has certain innate psychic skills and a working knowledge of natural magic, as well as a certain type of Pagan belief. There are quite a few different styles of putting this into practice. (My own is described in my book *Hedge Witch*, published by Robert Hale.) Thirdly, and in connection with the events in this story, I am a priestess of the Goddess Mari, ordained by Olivia Robertson of the Fellowship of Isis, a worldwide organization devoted to the resurgence of Goddess worship and an honouring of all Goddesses of Love, Beauty and Truth, by whatever name They are known, in whatever culture, amongst people of any religion, creed, sex, age, colour, race or social status.

Here I want to say that, though I believe a complete return
to Goddess worship in the West, and in the world at large, to be
essential, I do not aim to proselytize about my own path nor
advocate the entire destruction of Christianity nor any other
mainstream religion, except in their present forms. As the
patriarchal faiths are at present, they are hurtful to individual
women and men and also to our relationship with other life
forms. However, I am sure that a *genuine* honouring of
Feminine Deity would transform all patriarchal religions,
including those Eastern religions where the bias towards the
Masculine is gentler, but still exists. Christianity, Judaism and
Islam would no longer exist, as we now know them, but would
be reborn as more compassionate teachings, without authoritarianism, misogyny and class hatred.

Christianity as we know it has been based on a man-made
philosophy, meaning a patriarchal and false mythology. It was
devised by distortion of what could have been a genuine
mythology, for political reasons, by men who wanted power. It
was then imposed by military action and outright persecution of
all who disagreed with it. The conversion of many Pagan communities at swordpoint has been well-described elsewhere
(especially in Monica Sjoo and Barbara Mor's *The Great Cosmic
Mother*), so I will not repeat it here. Likewise, the story of the
burning or hanging of around nine million Pagans and heretics
for so-called 'devil-worship' should now need no repetition.
This is not to say that there were not many places that wel-
comed Christianity, but history bears witness to the fact that
those who did not were often physically forced to or coerced by
threat. Our Native European spiritual traditions suffered the
same way as Native American ones did, but more completely
and at an earlier point in time. The Church then helped to create a culture based on fear of the body and of women (sensuality and woman being seen as synonymous), and exploiting as
well as oppressing women, children, animals and the Earth
Herself. I certainly do not believe that the Roman Catholic
church invented exploitation or patriarchy, but as an organization it was quick to express itself patriarchally and to become
power-based, wealthy and, at its most extreme, fascistic - deny-
ing, among other things, the human right to freedom of belief.

So what does any of this have to do with Christ?

I am asking this as a rhetorical question and assuming the power called Christ by Christians to be pure, good, transformative and healing, the same as or similar to that understood by modern Pagans as the presence of the God, who also gives of His own life force, for the sake of all new life - the pure givingness of the Masculine principle.

One cannot help but warm to the personality of Jesus, as it is described in the New Testament. He seems to have been a remarkable man and a very great healer and storyteller. (For their wisdom and commonsense, the parables are extraordinary.) He said some very profound and interesting things. Though after all these years, and considering no one wrote about him, in the form of a gospel, until about sixty years after his death, it's obviously difficult to know just what he did say. (How clearly would you remember the exact words of what someone close to you said sixty years ago?) Therefore, a great deal of what Jesus is said to have taught is actually other people's mythologizing or else mediumistically channelled by Christian saints. As such, it is as much of interest as anyone else's work of a similar nature. To say it is the last word (on anything at all) and based on an historic rendering of actual events and actual spoken words is ludicrous.

Also, there is a very different picture of Jesus presented in alternative gospels not included in the Bible because of the decisions of the Christian hierarchy, early on in church history. Included in these gospels are not only a sexual relationship with Mary Magdalene but teachings which, as Ean Begg points out in his book *The Black Goddess*, are not unlike those of Jungian psychology.

Perhaps the most anyone can say is that Jesus was a warmhearted and charismatic man, a generous healer and interesting teacher who believed his voluntary death was of benefit to humanity. In this, he was very like the Corn Kings before and after him. But however you look at it, Jesus did care deeply and nowadays must look on from whatever Inner Realm or domain he inhabits and weep tears of blood over what has been done in his name.

In spite of this, the real value of a transformed Christianity as creative mythology and as a religion with great potential emphasis on compassion and service still remains to be explored. And indeed it is being creatively developed by many people, whose lives the Dark Goddess - sometimes through the form of Mary Magdalene or an esoteric vision of the Virgin Mary and sometimes through feminism and an innate respect for the value of personal spiritual experience - has touched profoundly.

A great deal of modern writing on the Goddess so far, including my own, has dealt with Her three aspects of Maid Mother and Wisewoman, as expressed in the three phases of a woman's life - young, mature and then older. This is linked, very obviously through the menstrual cycle, with a woman's fertility and childbearing potential, showing the goddess manifested in Her creation.

MAID — pre-fertile time or before the birth of a child. Exploratory, inspirational. Time of learning, beginning, growth, blossoming. (Nowadays, 'before the birth of a child' is taken to mean not only before an actual baby but also before an established work.)

MOTHER — fertile and one who has given birth to physical children and/or has directed that same energy into other forms of creativity. Able to express herself in mature and passionate sexuality. Also able to direct and administer in her own home, or in a larger realm.

WISEWOMAN — post-menopausal and possessing the emotional honesty normally available to younger women during the menstrual period, but now ongoing. One who has life experience and wisdom, as well as some skill as healer or counsellor. Grandmother, or one who stands in that relation to younger people or who advises or teaches in some way.

These phases are seen as metaphors for aspects of the goddess because, in Pagan belief, She is immanent in woman. We are all, every life form, an aspect of the body of the Goddess, but in woman is revealed certain ways in which the Goddess is active, both metaphorically and in actuality. In other words, a certain cycle of Goddess energy is shown in women and made available to them as individuals, to express in their own way. When not disturbed by emotional anguish or physical imbalance, this cycle is connected with the Moon, many women menstruating when the Moon returns to a certain phase or, alternatively, each time she is in a particular astrological sign. Because emotional stresses and environmental factors have tended to dislocate many of us from our harmony with nature's cycles, it is now much harder than it once was to see how our own cycles are attuned to that silver light. Nevertheless, it is well attested to, both in mythology and in physical fact. One importance of this is to show how we are one with life's rhythms on a large scale. This connects us through the Moon's mythic and archetypal meanings as well as through her great elemental power, with the psychic realm, inwardness and thus with the Dark Goddess.

Other life forms with a different reproductive cycle than the human are also expressing the energy of the Goddess, in both Her Dark and Bright aspects, but in different ways in relation to the Moon's phases. Therefore, there is nothing final in terms of understanding the Goddess, in this linking of Her to Moon phases and so to human fertility and a woman's life story. However, it is valid and has the advantage of letting us know Her within our bodies, if we are women. Or, if we are men, within the bodies of our mothers and lovers. Men also experience the Moon's cycles, psychically and emotionally, and as a change in their own energy levels, in a direct way within themselves.

In terms of the Moon's cycles and the Goddess in woman, it follows this pattern: Waxing Moon - Maid, Full Moon - Mother, Waning Moon - Wisewoman.

But there is another aspect of the Moon and of Goddess and woman. This has been hinted at or discussed by many writers, but I believe we have still to reclaim and fully understand our connection with Her and Her action in life. Her influence extends either side of Her 'quarter' of the Moon's time and in fact represents one half of the cycle. This aspect is called the Dark or Death Goddess. She is actually the hidden face of the Mother of All Life, by which I mean the one great universal, feminine life-force, throughout all space and time, infinite and endless, the counterpart of the Father. Her other Self is called the Bright Goddess, the one who shines forth in manifest creation, the beauty of all living. The realm where the dead go, which is also the psychic realm of our own inner reality and the dream world, is the area of the Dark Goddess and is also the seedbed of new life. It is from the Inner Realm of the spirit that all manifest life comes, or rather is born. This is one of the great teachings of the Western Mystery Tradition. It is also demonstrated in human life. For instance, when we fall asleep and dream, withdrawing into a state of unconsciousness ruled over by the Dark Goddess of Inner Realms and psychic activity our waking life is prepared for, not only through rest but in the emotional, psychological and spiritual work we do in the dream world. Through our unravelling of daily confusions, confrontations with buried fears and breakthroughs into lucid dreaming and so resolution, we achieve changes in ourselves that affect our outer lives - a kind of rebirth.

Dreams that shape all our lives take place in darkness and unconsciousness, in the place where the soul is active. Children grow in the darkness of a woman's womb, content in the inner richness of this dream state. The seed of a new tree likes to be buried (though we call it planting).

This realm of the Dark Goddess has been called evil for we fear it as we fear death. But death is actually the matrix of life, being the great renewer and destroyer of the outworn, as well as the entrance to the spirit realm where the first causes lie. There are many kinds of death, too. These range from death of an old way of life, resulting in new challenges and opportunities (perhaps painful, but illuminating), through death of the sense of separation imposed by the ego, which results in liberation and a sense of communion, to actual physical death, which prepares a person for after-life esoteric teachings - or so we are taught by the more open-minded religious traditions - and allows reappraisal of the incarnation that has ended and preparation for a new life in a new body.

Most of all, as Kathleen Raine says in her book *Defending Ancient Springs*, the sacred always comes 'from that other world to which the dead go and from which they come'. I understand her to mean that our sense of the sacred is bound up with our feeling for the mysteries of the psyche and spirit. We experience these as immanent in Earth and ourselves, but they come from the 'within', where the dead live, our ancestors and all spirit beings.

I hope all this begins to show why the Dark Goddess is the Queen of the three great Mysteries - Birth, Sex and Death - and why we can look to Her for rebirth. This is because there can be no new way of life without a death of the old way, and in terms of physical reincarnation (in which I, like most Pagans and like the early Christians, am a believer) there can be no rebirth in a new young body unless the old and withered one dies first. The Dark Goddess's realm leads us from death to life.

I was shown by my inner guide how this looks - that is, how the realm of the Dark Goddess fits in with the other three aspects of the Goddess and how death leads onto a new life, both literally and metaphorically. All below the horizontal lines that crosses the Moon diagram (see overleaf) belongs to the Dark Goddess; all above it belongs to the Bright Goddess. This is because Otherworldly influence, from the Dark Goddess's spirit realm, is felt most easily by the old or the very young. In the prime of life, above the diagram's horizontal line, most people feel a lot further from psychic experience, more focused on getting and spending, or rearing children. (The exceptions to this are the 'Dark Moon people', the mediumistic types.)

There are some interesting paradoxes about the cycle as a whole. How can the Goddess of the Otherworld be so active in sexual passion and even conception, the domain of the Bright Goddess of physical life? How can a wisewoman, whose womb does not bleed anymore, show the emotional directness of the menstruating woman? A paradox is a mystery and therefore has great power for we cannot contain it, nor reduce it to a construct.

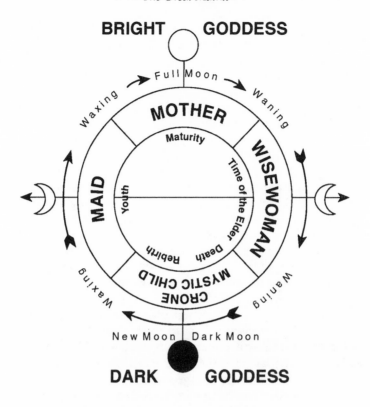

The Dark Goddess's phase of the Moon's cycle is that time when it is literally dark: from three days before the New Moon, then the day of the New Moon itself, when the tide turns from waning to waxing, then until the first frail crescent can be seen, about three days after the New Moon. Alternatively, She is the dark side of the whole Moon, while the Bright or White Goddess is symbolized by the Moon's visible face.

Though beginning as 'Crone' and 'Death', Her age varies in reverse order to that in the outer world, as She changes - and changes us - from ancient to younger and then to newborn, so that we emerge at the start of a new day (or new project or life). In cultures from around the world She is shown as ageless, sometimes appearing as very old, Her body worn and haggard, but often as much younger and strongly sexual and also as a very young woman. She may appear as a scavenger or mourner or visionary at the graveside, seeming sinister or beautiful: Kali, Erishkegal, The Morrighan, Mari, Isis - or Mary Magdalene at the tomb of Jesus.

The Dark Goddess's mythology, and presence, can be personally experienced by each one of us, yet very clearly is most transpersonal. For what could be more dissolving to and more beyond, as it were, the limitations of our separate personalities than death and death's realm, followed by rebirth? My belief, and a part of my particular message as a priestess, is that it is only through our most personal psychic experiences (of spirit presence, of intuition, of lucid dream, of sudden perception of the subtle, manifesting in art, of memories of our own past lives as either physical or psychological fact, of telepathy or synchronicity) that we can bring to each other and to life an understanding that transcends separation. That is why the story I am going to tell is about my own past lives and psychic experiences. I want to share them, as I have said, in order to encourage others to value their own knowledge and psychic perceptions. And also to describe ways in which past lives can be remembered and communion with the Dark Goddess attained by anyone. For these are accessible to each one of us. And they are ours by right, together with all the psychic sensitivity that we do have. They are also all that any one really has of psychic meaning in life. Without them, all scholarly analysis and metaphysics and all philosophy become just an intellectual exercise and are quite meaningless.

Recovering of personal memory of past lives and experiences of psychic communications with spirit beings will not make anyone's life a perfect dream of happiness nor confer any ultimate wisdom. My own life is as beset with human trials and tribulations as anyone else's. What I do have, what we can all have as women, is spiritual self-respect as a woman. What men can have, in sensing the Dark Goddess, is a knowledge of woman and the whole personal feminine realm as a transformative mystery, subtle and energizing, in addition to a sense of woman as spiritual comrade and sister, rather than as a chattel or demoness. What anyone can gain besides a deep sense of meaning in life, is a knowledge of personal spiritual orientation.

Resources to draw upon in times of trouble or, more happily, for healing and creativity. These are all from the realm of the dark Goddess, the inwardness or soul realm, and include help from or communion with inner spirit guides both human and non-human and, primarily, the Goddess Herself.

I need to say here that these benefits are gained whether or not one believes, for instance, that past life memories are real, in the sense of referring to something that physically happened to oneself while in another body. I believe that mine are, but there will be nothing in these pages that attempts to prove any such thing. Some past life memories are verifiable and there have been many accounts of people who were able to produce startling evidence that the facts they recalled as part of their own former existences were historically correct *and* could not have been known to them by any other means than the psychic. Arthur Guirdham's description of the memories of a group of reincarnated Cathars springs to mind most readily. There have been many other cases, both in the East, where such things are accepted, and in the West, where they usually are not.

My own past life memories do not contain much factual information which could be verified. This may not only be because some of these lives took place on a lost continent - Atlantis - but also because I am not a factually oriented person, not even in the present day. It must be admitted right from the start that I have no way of knowing if my memories are genuine or if they are produced by that aspect of me that could become a novelist. (I have often thought, since recall focuses on the dramatic moments, and not on the hours one spends doing chores or worrying or just waiting, that any one of them could have been expanded into a good novel!) However, this does not diminish their importance as individual mythology - my own - about my quest in life. And the same goes for anyone else's past or apparent past lives. I have also found that because I opened the door to these memories, I have been blessed with visions and teachings that do not need to be verified at all, because they speak for themselves and are truly profound. The same thing can be said of communications from my inner guides. They have helped me in understanding life. Whether they are being given by beings separate from myself, or by aspects of my own self becomes of secondary importance in comparison to this.

That survival after death and subsequent reincarnation are facts has been attested to in many other books. For me, the weight of the evidence is sufficiently convincing. But I do not claim here to be adding to that literature. Instead, I am presenting my story as an explanation of my contact with the Dark Goddess of a specific tradition and suggesting that it is creative for us all to take seriously our psychic and inner lives, including our far distant memories whether we feel the results are 'just' psychological, a valid spiritual experience of a personal kind or an objective piece of evidence for our survival after death. Or all three.

2

First Life and a Spirit Journey

I will start with a revelation, or rather a vision, about the origins of us all. For if I want to tell a story I should start at the beginning, and I cannot actually remember my very first life of all as an individual being. I think it is better, anyway, to look beyond this to the start of all life that exists, and to the deities who formed everything. (By deities, I mean the life force, in both its Feminine and Masculine aspect.) That not only shows the Dark Goddess in relation to the God, but puts all our subsequent lives in their real context.

A Vision of the Origins of All Life on Earth

I saw a dark sea on a dark night. There were no stars, yet a diffuse silver light shone and there were rocks on the beach and pale sand. I heard a voice say that in that first ocean, our own perfect potential was to be found - the being we could become at our finest and best, the Mother's original dream for our strength and happiness.

I knew that this ocean was not on our Earth but represented the great Sea of Space, wherein stars and planets and Earth would soon come to be. Yet it was not like the physical realm of the universe as we now know it, but an essence, a compacted image, a *possibility*. It was a dream of life.

Before this dream state was the dreamless sleep, in which

nothing was differentiated. This dreamless sleep was not Mother nor Father of Life but both. Then the dream arose naturally, just as our own dreams do. And behold! It was the Mother. She was both dream and dreamer. She carried within Her the Father God, who was Her twin brother. And now there was no dreamless sleeper containing all possibilities, but a realization, a dreamer and Her lover.

He arose from Her and I saw life in its origins. It appeared in this way:

Light came from the Dark Sea in a great serpent coil, spiralling - red-gold - upwards. It then turned and returned as a flash of lightning, re-entering the sea. Yet it also seemed to lay, gently like a red-gold mist, upon the face of the waters. Then I saw rise up from the sea all the galaxies and ours among them, and within ours many planets including our green Earth. She was rich with flowers and trees, birds and animals. Her rivers were full of fish and there were deep seas and high mountains.

I was told I was seeing Earth life, in particular, and its emergence from the Dark Sea, not because it is the only or best life in the universe but because I am from Earth myself.

I knew that I had just seen the passing of aeons, from the 'first' cold night of space to the earliest stars and then, through long ages, to our own planet's life, and later, to Her supporting of diverse life forms, a myriad of small lives.

And I knew also that there was no real beginning, as there would be no end. And that the creation of life is continuous, for the Mother gives birth anew, constantly, and that life is circular or a spiral, not a straight line with a start and a finish. Creation goes round, as nature's cycles show. It does not go from end to end. But when it arrives back where it seems to begin, it is upon a new arc, or in a new time span. The dreamless sleeper must rest, over and over again, though whether that is for a fraction of a moment or long ages I could not know, since time does not exist in that phase of creation. Then, each time, a new life is dreamt into being. It is useless, in a sense, to ask why, for it is the nature of the sleeper to begin dreaming. Yet the Mother dreams to a purpose, She dreams of happiness, of perfectly realized beings . . .

Then the vision of the Earth vanished and the waters were dark again. I waited, and was rewarded with a second vision that clarified the first. I was drawn right in to the process, to become at one with it in my astral body, for I suddenly was floating upon the waters on a gigantic green leaf.

I heard a voice say, Water seeks always the lowest level and she flows down to it. Water is our Mother. In this movement of Hers, there is mighty power. And the God, because of Her movement, separates Himself from Her. However, She does not create Him. Though She comes into being first and carries Him within Her, yet They are brother and sister. Originally They are at one and twined together more closely than the right and left sides of one single body. He is the fire power that Her movement generates, when churning against the wheel of nothingness - which is the Reverse Side of the Great Wheel of Life, the wheel of not being, of not having body nor any astral nor spiritual existence. She thus creates a challenge for Him and He answers by separating from Her and coming in to individual being as energy, the first fire. She first comes into being as a power of dreaming that is like a dark sea. By Her flowing, which is natural to Her, Her husband/twin brother arises from Their undifferentiated existence in which They knew neither separation nor a genuine union for They were not distinct enough from one another to unite.

After separation, He is able to act with Her, to blend His essence and power of life with Hers. This was the meaning of the light coming from and returning to the water, followed by the appearance of all the galaxies and all life forms. He had fertilized Her dreams and so She gave birth to worlds.

Be it understood that these are symbolic statements, drawn from the imagery of human experience and knowledge, to describe subtle mysteries.

I sailed on, upon the green leaf, and was swept, hurtling over and downward yet all the while safe, on a dark waterfall. At the bottom, I arrived in an immense white sea and sailed on again, still upon the green leaf. The flow took me between massive black rocks that rose up from the white sea, then down over another waterfall to an ocean of violet. Soon I had traversed all the waterfalls, sailing a sea of each colour of the rainbow; violet, indigo, blue, green, yellow, orange and red. The final waterfall tipped me onto a sunlit beach in our own world. I was in a visionary counterpart of our own Earth, an unspoilt Earth that was pristine and beautiful. The same I had seen rising up from the Dark Sea, as the Mother's pure dream for our Earth life.

A voice said that the Goddess and God love each other, eternally. The Mother and Father of Life mingle with each other as Water and Fire, the elements achieved by the first separation, because They desire to.

Here I must comment that there are other aspects of the Goddess as well as of the God. Thus, there are Fire, Earth and Air Goddesses, as well as Water ones and Goddesses connected with particular life principles and with planets. The same goes for the Gods. But, to quote Dion Fortune's famous saying, in reality 'All the Gods are one God and all the Goddesses are one Goddess.' It is not just as simple as female-water-Goddess and male-fire-God. However, in the vision I was shown (as opposed to other people's visions) the original primordial Goddess's nature was an inner or etheric equivalent of water. And the God's primordial nature was an inner equivalent of fire. Other aspects of each one of Them came later on.

Remember, visions of this kind are metaphors. If you arrive at what feels like a genuine truth about life's origins, in a metaphysical or mystical sense, but through a different system of symbolism than what is shown here, then that is just as valid as anyone else's. One of the things that I like about the Goddess tradition and Paganism is precisely that there is no final word nor ultimate vision. In this, it is like (in its practice through either ritual or inner, visionary experience) the writing of poetry, or like any art form. The symbol systems may change and be drawn from many sources, but all are valid, in some way or another, even though truth is a constant (but too paradoxical to be expressed in human constructs).

To continue. Water and Fire together make a rainbow. This is the rainbow arc that links our world with Otherworld places and beings. Along this arc we, and everything, flow into manifestation or make manifest our first unconscious impulses. As spirits, the last ocean in which we find ourselves, before coming into full physical being, is the salt sea of our individual mother's womb. And, of course, the First Ocean of Space where the rainbow begins is not really 'up above us' located in a higher place, nor even in a lower one. It is the vast and yet mysteriously untraceable centre. Life comes from within, and moves outwards.

Now, in this present time we are all living in, we are so far from the central Source of All Life that it is hard not to fall into error and ill-conceived action. Loss of inner communion with the Goddess and God (as the principles of the Vision of Beauty that Could Be and also of Love) is what causes all suffering and evil. And this loss is inevitable for all beings, though not constant, for an inner communion is sometimes regained. It is a result of separating from the original oneness of all things into a multiplicity of individual entities. It is not merely caused by the gaining of consciousness in a human sense, for cruel suffering exists among animals, as does violent competition. However, cruelty seems accentuated in mankind, whose sense of separation is extreme, into a refined and deliberate malice and capacity for torture that gives humans an extra experience of evil, beyond the animal. (No doubt this is shared by other intelligent life forms, as is our capacity for goodness. We are not alone in the universe.)

The purpose, I was told, of this separation out into manifestation is a great transformative magic. By separating Themselves from Their first state of being, the Goddess and God, manifesting in multitudes of separate beings, in all Their creation (as well as remaining transcendent within Inner Realms), the Goddess and God can reach complete fulfilment in loving union and total realization of beauty and happiness. They can live out the dream. This fulfilment is only possible if a separation, with all its attendant suffering, takes place first. That is, you cannot come together in loving union with another being unless that being is distinct from your own self - and so prey to the risk of falling into conflict. The dynamic union of opposites, of different forces, requires *two*. The coming together may be sexual, and just as it may be between lovers of the opposite sex so it may also be between lovers of the same sex, for difference is not only a matter of physical gender. Or the union may be non-sexual and sisterly or fraternal. Or it may be simply a psychic response based on mutual love, an emotional bond. It can even be the relationship of the craftsperson with her materials or the gardener with the earth, or the devotion and loyalty between a human and an animal. Love is love, no matter how it manifests. Regardless of how it expresses itself, its effect is transformative, returning us, bit by bit, to harmony, but changed. It heals the wounds of evil and suffering brought into being by the very conditions which made itself possible. The power of attraction and love is channelled into all kinds of creativity, so beauty and manifest happiness can exist along with fulfilment and realization of love.

In pre-conscious entities, like stones and plants, love is a raw elemental magnetism which bonds the different forces and powers of changing life forms. But even in these, it is said, nature spirits live who are motivated by their own intense passions, in their non-human dimension of life.

Fulfilment and realization of love in harmony and manifest beauty, the world where the fox shall lie down with the hare, or the lion with the lamb, takes all time and all life forms to bring about. The Feminine impetus behind this in our living world is the Bright Goddess. She is that aspect of the Mother who lives in physical fulfilment and creative action, bestowing happiness. Her sister and other Self, the Dark Goddess, remains Otherworldly, Goddess of the Spirit Realm from which we derive our sense of the sacred and to whom we go when we die, or sense in inner communion while we live.

In our lives on Earth, we must all return to the Dark Goddess over and over again, through sleep and death and in meditation. This gives us the refreshment we need, through contact with Her power and movement. These states of being have their own momentum, as She does.

To the Dark Goddess we must return, not forgetting also to honour Her partner, the loving God. One way to deliberately achieve this return, without experiencing either sleep or physical death, is to mediate upon the Sea Goddess (by whatever name - Tiamat, Marah, Cleito, Isis, Brighid, Mari-Morgan, etc. She can also be seen as universal Moon, the ruler of all tides.

Anyone can explore this visionary place. The Dark inner Sea can be reached quite simply. Begin by sitting quietly and free from interruption. You can be sitting upright in a chair, with your arms and legs uncrossed, or lying flat on your back on a bed (if you do not think that, lying down, you will just fall asleep). Next, you should attempt to relax, fully. Breathe deeply and rhythmically for a little while; then, as you lose interest in this, imagine that your eyelids feel very heavy, as heavy as on first waking. It would be an enormous effort to lift them. For some reason, this relaxes the entire body. If at first you do not get good results, try lifting them slowly a few times - then, once again, let them stay closed.

Now you should make an invocation for protection and for assistance on your inward journey. You could say this, or something like it in your own words :

'Dark Mother of All Life and All-Father of the Cosmos, I ask to be led, in vision, to your realm. I ask to be shown there the First Sea of Life. And to be given all the understanding I need about life's beginnings and also your original purpose for me, as an individual being within life's whole body. May guardian spirits assist me. May I be protected.'

See yourself standing upon a very high cliff at night. The bottom is so very far away that you can't even see it. It is a drop of phenomenal, awe-inspiring immensity. Before you are all the bright stars and blackness of near space and beyond that, away, much further than you can see, stretches infinity. You call upon the Dark Mother for assistance in your travelling, invoking Her power to help you to reach the great First Ocean. A winged creature appears close to you. It may be a white mare or a huge bird, or something else. Perhaps with some trepidation, you mount and are carried off, leaving the cliff-top very far behind you, and crossing space so fast that the stars blur. The winged one sets you down on a beach by the Dark Sea - then flies away. You call upon the Dark Mother and your spirit guides to show you what you need to see, then wait for what happens.

From now on, the vision is your own. Your inner guides and guardians will assist you, even if you do not know them and have not made any conscious contact with them. Call back the winged creature when you want to return to your starting point on the cliff-top, by asking for a return journey, in the Mother's name. 'May I be taken back, as I was brought here, both swiftly and safely.' Alternatively, you may find that the trance unfolds in its own way, bringing you back from the Dark Sea by some other method. Close with these words before opening your eyes, or with something like this :

'I give thanks to the Dark Mother and the All-Father, for what I have seen and understood. And to the guardian spirits for their assistance. May I now safely return to the everyday world, protected by this symbol and filled with inner strength.' Here you should visualize, above your head, a symbol you can associate with love and wisdom. This might be a five-pointed star or an ankh cross or a red rose. Or the equal-armed cross of the four elements of manifest life, surrounded by the Goddess's circle of infinity. This is a symbol far older than its Christian applications, so it may be used by unorthodox Christian and Pagan alike. Or you may have some symbol of your own, suggested by an inner guide.'

Afterwards, do not try to do anything requiring focused concentration, like driving a car, too soon. Instead, enhance a return to normal waking consciousness by some kind of gentle physical activity - eating, or strolling in the garden, or stroking the cat.

What follows may seem like a digression from the subject of my spiritual autobiography as priestess of the Dark Goddess, or from teachings about Her. But I must explain both the techniques and pitfalls of inner work. So I should like to add here some words of caution about trance. I am not one of those people who believes that all areas of the Inner Realm are all sweetness and peace. The astral and psychic realms are inhabited by benevolent guiding spirits and elementals, mediators of the Goddess or God. Some of these are discarnate humans and some are other life forms or nature spirits. However, this realm interacts with human imagination and contains unpleasant entities (distorted 'thought forms' and visualizations empowered with destructive energies) as well as our 'good dreams' and the spirit guides. And just as everything that glitters is not gold, so all that appears to be helpful and wise is not always so. Therefore, when you see a being to whom you wish to relate, like the winged horse or the huge bird, visualize yourself holding a mirror towards it, the reflecting face towards the other being. Nothing false can bear to see the truth of itself. So if what you are encountering is an unhelpful being, it will at this point turn away and disappear. Look around you and see if there is another winged being (or whatever it is you have just called upon) and try again. True guides and helping spirits have emotional honesty about themselves - and courage and integrity, so they do not fear to look at their own reflection, even if it contains some weakness.

There are also destructive spirits who are not human thought forms in any way, but of a different order of being than ourselves. Mischievous nature spirits and cruel elves are among these, as opposed to the gentle nature spirits and the kind elves, whom you are much more likely to meet. They are life forms less materially dense than we are and belong to that part of nature which is normally invisible to us. They have been called 'supernatural', but they are not 'above' nature, for nothing is. The false opposition of Nature to Spirit is an insidious, damaging aspect of patriarchal spirituality, but is no part of the Goddess tradition! Worshippers of the Mother Goddess know Spirit is Nature's inwardness and Nature is Spirit's manifestation, only showing conflict and brutality because the Spirit, in its appearance in this everyday world, has emanated and translated itself far from the pure Source of All Life, the sphere of the first deities, of necessity.

In reality, nature is larger and more mysterious than we have been taught, and contains other dimensions than the world of the five senses. And if you begin by building, through visualization, your chosen inner scene, and accompany that with an invocation of deities and spirits, requesting them to help you, you may find that not only those beings you have called upon come to you, but also some you have not. You have gone to the borders of the Otherworld and there raised up your voice, attracting their attention. Most of the spirits who come to you as a result will be helpful, but some will not. I myself believe in the principle that 'like draws to like' and that some 'wicked spirits' we see correspond to weaknesses in our own characters. This is where magical-psychic work overlaps with the modern forms of psychotherapy that include inner techniques like visualization. We can work upon healing ourselves and the 'wicked spirit' by identifying them with each other in a healing continuum that benefits both parties. But such issues are different from the ones you would work with in trances such as I have just described. In this trance, the aim is to get in touch with the Dark Mother's first dream, Her pure conception of how life can be, both for our own individual selves and also, when fullest potential has been reached through love's healing power, for the whole world.

Perhaps I should go back to my comments about creatures such as elves and explain why they are not always helpful. It is because they, too, are separated from the Life Source, being individual entities as we are. Folk lore abounds with instances of their not always benign actions and attitudes, and this is because they can suffer from the various forms of psychic sickness that stem from a loss of contact with the deities, even while living within a dimension of the Otherworld, or having, as it were, a foot in both worlds. Mischief is not a sickness and may serve a good purpose. Malice is another matter, however, and could lead to your being shown false visions or given inaccurate guidance. There is no need for alarm, as all these beings will respond in the same way to 'being mirrored'. Caution is a good idea but fear is unjustified.

How much or little you may see of the Inner Realm beings of any kind, at first, and how much guidance you will actually hear depends on the present state of your psychic senses. You may be someone who has worked as a witch, priestess or priest, enchantress or bard, or in some capacity where your skills were developed, in former lives. You may have been born clairvoyant or clairaudient, notwithstanding that the lack of their use can make these skills rusty. On the other hand, this may be the first life in which you have done very much of this kind. Either way, as with any other quality or skill, the more we use it the more it gains strength. Regular practice of psychic skills will soon develop them. But it does much more for the confidence of any one of us to value the glimpses and the guidance that we do get, rather than pointlessly to moan at ourselves for not being more psychic. Modern life has encouraged us to value the 'hyped-up' and the over-dramatic, or unconsciously to measure our psychic skills against those of Hollywood magicians and stage mediums in films about the so-called supernatural. Real psychic experiences are usually far more subtle than that. However, trances like the return to the Dark Mother's Sea can be seriously challenging for a beginner, so I shall be covering a way of developing our psychic faculties later in this book.

For now, I just want to mention the first and best way to deepen psychic perceptions. Pay very close attention to their faint whispers. Let yourself notice things like a brief feeling of inner knowledge about someone's feelings or a warning voice about some project, or feelings of unease or optimism for which there are no apparent grounds, or 'astral blessings', even if these arrive and fade almost before you can turn to them. (Among 'blessings' I include feelings of being spontaneously healed of some sickness while seeming to be quite alone, spirit messages giving helpful advice, wonderful smells of incense or flowers or perfume from no known physical source, inner communications or foreknowledge concerning family or friends, etc.) When this kind of thing happens, most of us have been taught to dismiss it as fantasy or illusion and warned not to get caught up in a world of superstition, or even worse, madness! And it is true that there are mentally ill people who hear many inner voices, some of which may be aspects of themselves and some the Inner Realm spirits their condition has attracted. Sometimes they are told to do self-destructive things by the voices, or are even told to injure others. But if you are not mentally ill in the first place, you will not become so by paying attention to your inner voices. And you will not start doing weird things because of visions and spirit voices, since any instruction can be checked against common sense.

For instance, if a spirit voice told you to step off a cliff, you would obviously be crazy to obey the instruction. A sensible response would be to assume that the cliff-top may have been the site of previous suicides and that you are hearing the instructions those people gave to themselves. In such emotionally intense situations, a psychic imprint can be left behind - not always a haunting, exactly, but a kind of record. You might also consider the idea that you are feeling self-destructive. On another occasion, however, you might be warned to take a different route than your usual one going home. Then you'd have nothing to lose by taking the advice, since it can't hurt you and may mean you avoid some accident or attack.

Common sense is a wonderful thing and so is scepticism. Neither one should be thrown out the window - and needn't be - simply because you start letting your own inner senses speak. But the value of listening is that you will gain extra information. For instance, if you should hear an inner voice or smell something bodiless, see if you can find out more. Watch with your inner eye (your 'mind's eye') for accompanying images. Feel in your body what sensations come to you. Turn your attention that way, rather than away! The messages, in time, will amplify if you do this and will help you in making decisions and in gaining understanding of life.

The purpose of all this is just what it has always been: inner strength in times of trouble and increased understanding of where we fit into the whole scheme of things. And enhanced creativity. The gifts of the Dark Goddess, whose realm is the psyche.

3

The Linking of Love and Prophecy

I have wondered how to structure the episodes in this story I want to tell. Should I describe the past lives and revelations in the order in which I learned of them? But this could be as confusing for others as it was (frequently at the time) for me! I have decided, instead, to tell of events in their actual chronological order, though accompanying comments, teachings and ideas will often have the benefit of hindsight and be based on what I know now. The first incarnation that I shall relate is one that happened around 11,000 or 12,000 years ago.

Certain unexplained discoveries (sometimes known as 'fortean phenomena') indicate that there was human life on Earth a very long time before historians or archaeologists have acknowledged it.

For instance, in an open-cast coal mine in Australia three discs were found in 1977, encased in what appeared to be rusted metal. They were said by a marine expert to be millions of years old, so far as anyone could tell, and of unknown purpose They definitely were not fossilized shells. (This was reported in the book *Fortean Times*, edited by Paul Sieveking.) The discs were identical in size and perfectly circular.

This, and other recorded but little known instances of similar phenomena, shows that we may be very far wrong in our estimate of when human life (or something else that was like it) first appeared on this Earth.

I am relating these things to indicate just how incredibly

recent my far memories actually are, since the furthest back I can remember is on the continent of Atlantis, and not even at the beginning of that culture's history.

The date that I was given was 'seven thousand'. At first, I thought this meant 7,000 B.C.E. (Before Common Era). By many people's reckoning, this would be after Atlantis's end, so it may have meant 7,000 years since some important Atlantean event. Some authorities believe that Atlantean culture lasted from about 15,000 to 8,000 B.C.E. and few give the date of its ending as later than around 6,000 B.C.E., while most assume an earlier date. In any case, it was not all that long ago, not even when you compare it to the dates of paleolithic human culture, let alone to the signs indicating that human life may have been here many millions of years back

My first memory of Atlantis was of a time before corruption, a kind of golden age of that culture's life and certainly, for me, a time of great spiritual realization, untrammelled by any feeling of the decadence which was to come.

The whole question of Atlantis is fascinating. Most people know the story in brief, but for those who do not, I will recount it. Atlantis is believed to have been a lost land, a whole continent, situated in what is now the Atlantic ocean. It is a legendary 'drowned land' and said to have been submerged beneath the ocean after some kind of geological catastrophe which was brought on by misuse of the strong Atlantean magic, a kind of techno-magic exploitative of the Earth and disturbing to nature.

Some researchers now believe that the Earth could have been undergoing a natural geological change, concurrently with Atlantean goings-on, and that the continent would have been wiped out anyway independently of any damage caused by humans. In any event, Atlantean society at the end of its days was ruled by men whose main aim was power for power's sake, and who were prepared to make use of other people and of natural resources for their own gain and without care for the consequences.

But did it ever really exist, or is it 'only' mythical? What, therefore, do we mean if we say that we 'lived' there?

As far as I know the first impetus for the story of Atlantis comes to us from the writings of the Greek philosopher Plato. It is backed up by the revelations of many gifted psychics and also in oral tradition from some tribal cultures. There is archaeological evidence for its reality, in the shape of ruins found under the waters of the Atlantic. There are also known to be some geological indications, like land under the sea showing formations that can only occur in what has once been above water.

As far as I am concerned, it was a real place. But it is also a legendary land, about which people weave many hopes, fears, dreams, imaginings and longings, just as they do about ancient Egypt or even present-day Ireland. I believe my story is real and really happened, but I also believe it is worth sharing just as a dream or a poem would be, not solely as a manifest happening in historical context.

My guides tell me that nowadays Atlantis is not only mythical but also has become, in a certain sense, the place where any former Atlantean is now living. Atlanteans bring some of the essence of lost Atlantis (hopefully at its best) to wherever they are. So Atlantis can now be almost anywhere. This shows some of the action of the Dark Goddess, how the death of Atlantis as a physical location has translated it into other spheres! And perhaps, in time, its pure, uncorrupted heyday will be reborn, not on the stretch of land now under the Atlantic but elsewhere in the world, with the best of its principles lived out in forms compatible with those of other cultures.

It was, in its own historical time, a most variable place, the sublime overtaken by the downright evil. And it always had, of course, its share of the ordinary and banal, as all places do. But in Atlantis a dream was almost realized for quite a long time - and a good understanding was once reached there between the masculine and feminine.

My Atlantis or yours? People's actual memories of it do differ a lot. This is because it was a *big* place, an entire continent, larger than Libya and Asia, according to Plato, though this may be an exaggeration on the part of his informant. It seemed to consist of a group of islands, with one main island, and its history spanned many thousands of years. One has only to look at the difference between present-day London and a medieval town in France and a village in Denmark about 100 C.E to realize that future recall of lives in what we now call Europe could produce startlingly different images. And in 10,000 years time, people may not know enough, historically, to understand how the different pictures fit together. Therefore, dear fellow Atlantean reader, if your memories of the lost continent are not like mine, differing hugely in regard to dress fashions, religious beliefs, style of architecture or political climate, that is because life on Atlantis was diverse and varied, even in similar locations and in the same decade! Think of present-day South America, where Amazonian Indians still live in neolithic and tribal style while nearby there are vast and vastly polluted modern cities.

The time that I can recall was one of religious sophistication and refinement of spiritual concepts, in a temple culture of some complexity. There were also, as the opening of my story shows, people living then with quite primal beliefs and their own sort of sensitivity.

An Account of the Memory of a Life in Atlantis, as a Priestess of Meri of the Tides

I was living with nomads by a beach in Atlantis, beside an open, shallow bay. I seemed to be about fourteen or fifteen years old, but could not be exactly sure of my age. This was partly because, in the nomadic culture in which I had been brought up, people did not keep count of the passing of the years. We had skin tents, like archetypal Bedouins, but the tribe had features like modern southern Europeans, and dark hair. Women wore dresses of small, square patchwork pieces sewn together, in colour combinations like orange, pink and brown, with the bright colours predominant. Men wore black and 'white' (or unbleached cloth).

I knew I was not one of the nomads myself, not one of their tribe, but I had lived with them for most of my life. They told me I had been found by them on the beach as a baby and had certain possessions which showed me to be the child of a temple priestess. These possessions included a collection of what looked like silver charms, threaded on a black leather band, and a pack of beautifully hand-decorated cards - like a modern Tarot pack but with different designs. The nomads kept showing me a particular card, a picture of a woman dressed in white and gold and seated on a throne, holding a white flower that could have been a lily. They said this was my card, though I didn't know why.

The nomads also told me I looked different from them, that my face was shaped differently with almost sallow skin and that my hair was darker and denser than their own. The only other things that I remember from this first glimpse was that across the bay from us there was a large city of glittering white buildings, but I had never been there. On our wanderings, the tribe avoided cities.

Moving forward to the next important time in my life, which I think was only a matter of months later, I found that I was waiting alone in the tent that I lived in, for a man to come to me. This was a kind of rite of initiation, or rather it was part of one. Someone - but I was not to be told who it was going to be - would come in and make love to me. For these people loss of virginity was an organized rite, disconnected from marriage or personal love. It was seen as entry into a kind of power, a gain rather than a loss.

I waited with some nervousness, hoping very much it would be someone I liked! But no man came to me. After a lot more waiting, I drifted into a sort of daze. Eventually, I was called back outside. The people were sitting cross-legged on the Earth, in a large group. An old tribal wisewoman then explained that all the men were frightened of me, because of where I had come from, which was believed to be the city across the bay, and because of the strange magical powers they thought I had and which they saw as different from those of their own wisewomen or wisemen. So far, I had shown no particular signs of anything magical at all. I had merely tried to blend in and to win their forgiveness for being unlike them. But they felt strongly about the mysterious temple charms and cards that were found with me.

About an hour or so later, I was alone with a black-haired

man, who looked about thirty-five years old. I knew that, in a fatherly sort of way, he was very fond of me, and had taken a special interest in my upbringing. He said that, as I already knew, it was thought that my mother had been a temple priestess, but it was not known why she had abandoned me. Perhaps she had drowned. This heritage, and the strange circumstances under which I was found, had made me a child of the Goddess in their eyes. Not simply in the way that we are all children of Goddess and God, but something more than that - singled out. That was why no man would mate with me. They all feared the consequences of a union of that kind. I was holy and - as a result - taboo. So I couldn't stay with the tribe any more, explained my dark-haired 'father', apologetically and with sadness. I had to leave. This was because I could no longer live their life and keep their customs. Really, it would be for the best if I left that night.

I stared at him, horrified, too stunned to be tearful. I had known no other life than with the nomads. To me, they were family, friends, country - they were all I had!

My 'father' seemed sorry to part with me, but would not go against the wishes of the people. He explained that he had really hoped that some young man would overcome his fear. In fact, the elders of the tribe had all agreed that if this happened, it could be taken as a good omen for my continued presence among them, a sort of sign. But nobody had.

I asked if I could say goodbye to the woman who had acted as my tribal mother, and the 'sister' I shared a tent with and all my friends. He said, no, much better not to. He gave me a stick, the charms and the cards and told me to go to the city on the far side of the bay, which was a whole city of temples, and look for the one these cards had come from. The city was called Ruta.

I went on my way in the dark, with the stick and my possessions. I cannot remember whether, in that part of the continent at that time, there were predatory animals to fear, because I was then too upset to give the matter any thought. My feelings were outraged, even though I understood nomadic customs so well that I could see quite easily why they had done this. Eventually, with the comparative resilience of youth, I decided to look forwards instead of back. After all, they had always told me that I was different. If I wanted a feeling of belonging, which I did, much better to look to the place I was walking to than yearn for the one I had left. Perhaps the people there would be more accepting of me. I walked hard and fast.

In the early morning, I arrived. I was on the edge of the city. None of the nomads ever went inside it, so I knew nothing about it. All the buildings were white and plain and simple, but very large, and shining in the early light. Though white, they were not matt, but a sort of crystalline. Some were three or four storeys high and I saw one street built as a crescent (though not like the Regency crescents I know in Britain. The buildings were simpler, almost like village architecture in Greece, but on a huge scale.)

There was no one at the city's edge except a man whom I took to be a priest, walking swiftly towards me. I showed him my cards and asked my question. Which temple do I need? I explained that I was looking for my mother's people. He wrote the name of the Goddess down for me - Meri - and spoke it aloud, saying I needed Her temple. He gave me the paper to keep. The script on it looked Roman. (The reason why it was like this was explained to me later, by my inner guide, because I asked about it. Since the answer formed part of some lengthy teachings - too much to include here - I'll come back to this later on.)

The man explained that I must receive a kind of purification before going into a temple. He was concerned that I had just 'walked in'. Apparently, people didn't do that in those days. You came into this city of the temples either by invitation or by prior arrangement, after making a formal request, and for a specific purpose. The small town or village 'chapels' were not enclosed like this, but the city of the temples was 'set apart'. In practice, there were a great many visitors for many reasons, but no one was meant to just walk casually in!

I told him my whole story and he became quiet and thoughtful. I liked him, though he was quite a lot older than myself, and so carried the intimidating atmosphere of authority. His robes were entirely black and he had a short beard. He told me I would have to wait for a while on the beach before I came in.

The sun was just coming up then - the bay faced east. I waited all that day. At nightfall, when I was very tired, hungry and weak, not having eaten for a long time and having been through a great deal, he came back to me bringing food and drink. There was also a letter of introduction to the chief priest, which he had written himself, telling a half-truth about me - that I was a pilgrim known to him and in need of healing. He said that I could tell my story a bit later on, when people knew me better. He gave me a green dress to put on too.

Later, I went down a panelled passageway into a big hall. It had a tiled floor, very large tiles of black and white and perhaps made of marble. There were lots of priests and priestesses in biscuit-coloured top robes, with a black under robe and a thin white one. One priest was all in black, with a tall hat very like a modern chef's hat. He was the chief priest. He read my letter, and then I was in! He directed me through a door and told me to go down some stairs to a big underground room with a pool in it. This was fed, along a channel, by seawater. I had to get in and immerse myself, which was the purification that the young priest had mentioned. Afterwards, I spent time with priestesses robed in green, receiving healing.

In fact, I spent some months with this same healing and teaching group, learning the ways of the temple and receiving instruction. (It appeared that although the temples could be quite hard to get into, no one would really question a person 's presence once they were in and wanted to stay.)

Eventually, I decided to trust a priestess with my story. She took me outside onto the beach to meet another woman - a priestess of Meri of the Sea Tides. (The green-robed priestesses seemed to work from another aspect of Meri or it may have been from another Goddess. Sadly, I cannot recall all the details about this.) The priestess of Meri of the Tides was robed in blue. Her features were what I would now call 'far eastern' or perhaps Malaysian. I do not mean that was where she came from but that she looked like that. In fact, the priests and priestesses of the temple city had features showing an origin in many parts of the continent, or even, quite possibly, in other continents. This one had dark hair and yellow-brown skin, like my own, whereas the priestess in green was fair-haired and pale.

The priestess of Meri had a crystal ball, which she took from her pocket, and called a 'small moon'. It was made of whitish yet slightly transparent crystal. She asked me to look into it and say what I saw.

When I looked the inside of the crystal seemed to become vast. I was looking at a whole ocean inside it, in which a whale swam. This huge whale I knew to be a messenger of Meri. Then the whale swam away and the whole scene changed - for a tidal wave rose up and drowned the temple city and all around it. All the people were drowned. Then I saw another time in the future, long after the drowning, in a land I didn't recognize. There were the people again, but they all had bodies which emanated a rainbow light, and they walked among trees.

I saw in the crystal that Atlantis and all the trees and animals and people had all been given birth to by the Goddess, whose messenger and mediator had appeared to me as the great whale. This going beneath the waters and arising anew was a part of what it meant to be alive. It was part of the processes of fate that were set in motion simply by the existence of Creation. As humans, we could transcend fate or change its direction, but this would mean voluntary immersion in the spiritual waters of Meri, for all people of the future. Then the going under and arising would be without fear.

All this I told to the priestess of Meri, though without fully understanding what it meant.

She was astonished that I had seen this and talked rapidly to the priestess in green, arranging to take me straight to the Temple of Meri from the House of the Pilgrims. Evidently, it was thought that my success in divination with the 'small moon' indicated the probable truth about who my mother was - a temple priestess of Meri. Of course, they knew that a mother and child had disappeared about fifteen years ago and that I was of the same racial type - and possessed temple cards. The two priestesses conferred about this. No one else in the temple yet knew about my claims to be actually the disappeared temple child, except for my friend, the priest. And it was hardly likely anyone would make up a story like that! Yet the priestesses knew that they would be held partly responsible by temple authorities if there were some mistake or fraud. Were they going to believe me? It seemed that my prowess with the crystal had convinced them. The vanished priestess had had the same skill, to a high degree. (In fact, all the priestesses of Meri were chosen for their skill in prophecy and 'word-magic', but innate talent still varied.) It was believed that the quality and type of vision - rather than simply the faculty of clairvoyance, which many of the nomads and other people possessed - was what really clinched it. This was not seen as real proof that I was the missing priestess's daughter, but as one reason too many why I could not be dismissed.

Soon, I was robed all in blue and walking on the beach, with another priestess of Meri. I was holding a stone egg, of the same crystal as the stone moon. The priestess asked me, 'Do you know why this egg shape is linked with the Moon?' Then she explained to me about cycles of women's fertility and the Goddess in all things that are Moon-ruled, like the tides of the ocean. Much of this was similar to concepts I had been taught among the nomads. But she went on to say that our wombs are inner oceans and that eggs originally 'came out of the ocean'. Eggs are female and so linked with the Moon.

Moving forwards from this, I was ordained as a priestess. I was taken to the beach in front of the temple and told to sit down in a star that was drawn there in the sand, a star with many points. This was at or just below the high tide mark. The Moon was coming up to the full that night. I was told that whatever happened, I must remain sitting inside the star, unless instructed otherwise. Another priestess, seeing I was nervous, said to me, 'Don't worry, we have all been through it.'

Then an elderly priestess gave me the stick that I had arrived with and told me to leave it behind inside the star, and to let the waves take it. I was also then given my own crystal egg to hold. My forehead was annointed with a thick, sweet-smelling cream. I was conducted into the centre of the star, then everyone else left. I was alone on the beach, as the night fell. The incoming tide moved steadily towards me, and on this theme of the tides I was meant to meditate. I was also to commune with the spirit of Meri, as She moved in the deep sea. The water was still some way off. I decided to lie down. The Moon had risen and Her light was falling across the sea and on the beach, too. I communed with the spirit of the Moon Goddess of Tides, through the power of that white light. (For us, Meri of Inner Tides was worshipped at Dark and New Moon. Meri of Outer Tides was present at Full Moon. Yet it was also understood that each aspect implied the other, as death implies life and life implies death.) She entered me completely, and I became one with Her. I stayed very still, while the tide came closer. The waves began breaking gently right over my feet, but still I lay entranced. I knew that the Lady who rules the tides is in everything that has ever been created. Ebb and flow, Her power is final. And we need to be in harmony with Her and 'ride the wave'. Then pale green light seemed to come to me from the Moon. I rose up astrally from my body and floated away into the dark sky. The temple and the whole city had gone, completely. There was nothing but the sea, just the ocean, in all directions. I felt very peaceful and content and knew myself as a part of all that lives, belonging and connected, not ever really separate either from Goddess or Her creation. The great whale swam by and I watched Her, and drifted, knowing I would not feel so happy if in my mortal body, yet perfectly at ease.

Suddenly the sky filled with a much darker green underwater light. I was right back in my body at once! And lying under the waves, weak and terrified. And then - blank - for I went unconscious. When I was conscious again I was further up the beach and soaking wet. The priest whom I had previously met had pulled me from the water. He had decided to stroll down to keep an eye on me, though he wasn't meant to do that. He lit a driftwood fire to warm me and said he would stay with me now, till the morning, when the others would return for me.

I asked him 'What happened?'

He said, 'No one expected you to lie down. You were told to sit up. If you had done so, you would have been all right. The star is placed so that at high tide the waters will not close over your head, unless you lie down. And no one thought you would do that! Whatever made you think of it?'

I replied, 'I only meant to do it for a little while. Then the Moon Goddess came to me and I was - sort of - held down.'

'No, of course you were not,' he said anxiously. 'It is just that in deep trance people can lose consciousness of their physical whereabouts. And you may have been powerfully affected by the herbs you were annointed with. You should never have decided to lie down in the first place. You were given quite clear instructions for your own safety.'

He became more gentle with me after he'd said that. He held my hand and gave me his own cloak, because I was shivering. I asked if anyone had ever really drowned during this part of the rite of ordination. He said that it was extremely rare. But because of the herbs and the individual's varying response to the powers invoked, it had been known. The sea sometimes did take someone to Her. Though this was never intended by the priesthood, it could happen.

'But did the sea want me? She would have taken me, as you put it, if you hadn't come. Does this mean that She wanted me? And what for, if She did?'

He looked at me, in silence.

Later, he gave me another crystal egg from his own pocket, as mine had been lost. Also, that night, he gave me a special book as an ordination gift. (I do not think by then that I had learned to read, but it was planned that I should.) The book was handwritten with wonderful neatness. He had been meaning to leave me undisturbed in the star, but from time to time, watch over me. In the morning, when the others returned, he had meant to come along too and give the book. As it was, he went away before dawn, promising to put the book somewhere safe until another time. He covered up traces of the fire, burying them in the sand. I returned to the star, from which the sea had now retreated somewhat, and just waited quietly. Apart from my friend and myself, no one ever really knew what had happened that night.

I was then put through other, more formal rites, for which this vigil had been a preparation.

Later, I was working as a priestess in the temple of Meri. The main room had many small sea-water pools, sunk down into the floor. The temple front gave immediately onto the beach and the main doors were left open except in very inclement weather. Thus, it was rather like being inside a sheltered area of rock pools. We lived, worked and worshipped the Lady of the Tides with the sea just yards away from us, and we were surrounded by sea scent and sound.

The inside of the main room was grand but not ornate. There were huge white pillars holding up the roof and walls mostly of the same white material. That is, they were all built of it, but in some places decorated with religious imagery in carved wood. The floor was of brown stone, semi-transparent, a kind of pale, brown crystal, rather like sand in colour, which was why it was chosen. At the back was a stone carving of a Full Moon shining over the sea. Below this, there were two wooden doors, decorated with carved fronds to look like seaweed. These led into a small inner sanctum, where there was another altar, on which a lamp was burning. (The main altar was below the carving of the Full Moon, but well forward from the doors.)

Much of my own work, which consisted of trance and meditation as well as ritual, was done on the beach (though not near the high tide mark!) and also in the temple. One of my tasks was the consecration of the sea-water pools and use of the water for healing purposes, as well as for annointing cups, candle holders and so on, that were used at the altar.

The pools were mostly kept clean by the wildlife in them, though I think from time to time they were cleaned out manually. The temple was far too high up the beach for the water to be replenished naturally, except in the event of severe floods! And there was no underground channel like that which fed the big pool in which people were purified.

I was, particularly, a priestess of whales and dolphins, because the Great Mother had come to me in trance in this form and also because it was felt that our temple was linked with them, and they were sacred.

I was instructed in how to mediate the Lady's blessing to dolphins in the sea and to heal any sick ones, since their presence in the oceans was magical and holy. They mediated to us a special joyfulness, too, and were helpful spirits on our psychic journeys into or across the ocean. It was not that we protected them or mediated to them while seeing them as somehow a lower life form than ourselves. In fact, it was felt strongly that they gave the Lady's blessing to us. And this was a two-way process. Our attitudes were not quite like those of twentieth-century Europeans. There was much less 'either/or' in the way we perceived things and more heartfelt embracing of paradox. Also, we knew much less separation between ourselves and other creatures than is felt now, and much more acknowledgment of their sacredness and mystery - in spite of the relative sophistication in which we lived.

The God who was worshipped then, as a counterpart of Meri, and whose priests the men were, was a God of the Fire in the Darkness and in the Deep or Underworld (dark, buried places and deep caves and under the ocean). He was not a Sun God but a kind of Plutonic deity, though understood as the All-Father, beneficent and life-directed, in contrast to the way that the Greeks seem to have depicted their God Hades or Pluto. His priests all wore black to denote the Underworld and Mystery. He was God of the Brightness in the Dark. Night, the powerful realm of His partner, the Goddess, was not seen as evil.

He was the vital electricity in life, or its spiritual equivalent. The Father God, who animates the Mother's darkness-from-which-all-life-comes. With Her, He was a primary creative power.

It was believed that from Meri, Lady of the Cosmic Tides and the Great Sea of Night, and Her Dark/Bright Lord who animated Her dreams, came other deities, like the Sun God, who was Their son. She ruled Death, Birth and conception, as well as Love. Most particularly, She ruled the inner psychic realms from which prophecy and all 'fate-speaking' came. (In this, as in most things, She was like other Dark Goddesses from around the world, in other times and cultures.) She was also Lady of Eternal Rhythms.

The God, who I think was called something like Ruar or Ruor, was able to animate all things by mysterious alteration of the pattern. She, the Lady of the Tides, was actually 'constancy', because you could always be sure that She would bring things back, in a constant ebb and flow. He was the bringer of crisis. We believed that He acted suddenly and without much warning. He was said to be potent in storms, and one of His major symbols was a flash of lightning. He helped Meri to create new life and His actions could promote healing. He was also, paradoxically, the watcher in darkness who stands guard over all who sleep.

Meri provided the clear dreams and visions which are life's beginning. Into these went Her essence of loving wisdom and of beauty and harmony. His action was to fertilize these dreams, so that She could make them real, that is, give them birth into full life. However, He did not help to actualize Her dreams without adding of Himself, to be actualized by Her. It was a reciprocal process, each providing the means for the other's equally vital originality to become realized. Neither one was seen merely as the agent or vessel or catalyst for the other's creativity. It is just that being a catalyst was a vital part of His action in the generative process. The qualities and attributes He had were perceived as being like those of Meri. He also was visionary, loving and wise. But the style in which this was emanated was Masculine, in complementary partnership with Her style of Feminine envisioning.

As a priestess of Meri, and a woman, I had far more to do with Her mysteries than those of the God and more knowledge about them. This does not mean that, in Atlantis in those days, the Feminine was valued at the expense of the Masculine. Neither does it mean an undervaluing. The power and the gifts of both Goddess and God were then acknowledged equally.

It will be seen by this that Atlantean spirituality, at this point, was very much based on what I would now call polarity. It was a balanced thing which honoured Goddess and God. Therefore, there was much interaction between priestesses and priests. However, in the temple of Ruar, which was also in the city, the priests were in control. Just as, in the Sea Temple of Meri, the priestesses ruled. Shared areas were open to both - and priests were often found in the temple of Meri, alongside female colleagues. In the same way, women went often to the God's temple. There was no feeling that celibacy was a virtue. It was seen as a perfectly acceptable choice, but sexuality was sacred, so sexual relationships often existed within the priest-hood.

These practices and beliefs were not heterosexist, for those able to mediate Goddess and God, in bisexual or homosexual orientation, were seen as possessing a particular kind of sacred understanding.

It was known that without Meri's visions, which gave Her the power to bring all through to birth, or rebirth, there would be nothing for the God to animate. But without Ruar's power to fertilize, Her dreams would be static and anything She gave birth to, as (we knew even then) some early life forms were pro-duced by parthenogenesis, would lack adaptability and strength. Above all, the great evolutionary leaps in the Lady's creation wouldn't be taken, because there would be no stimulus of fric-tion, no antithesis. But She was the Ground of All Being, while He was the outrider to New Ways.

Because the Masculine and Feminine were both valued, and also were seen as beyond maleness or femaleness in a human sense (including these but transcending them), beliefs did not lead to gender-stereotyping. Neither sex had more power than the other and people were valued, as individuals.

It is true that when I was seeking entrance to the city, my friend sent me to the High Priest. But this was because he was himself a priest and therefore this man was his own 'chief' and he knew his ways and was expected to refer to him in all mat-ters like this. If the first person I had encountered had been a priestess, I should have been interviewed by the High Priestess - though not all pilgrims met either of these people. I learned that later.

Though there were many rites based on or celebrating polari-ty, and involving both priestesses and priests, these were not directly sexual. There were no group orgies, as fertility rites, and no impersonal sex for religious purposes, arranged by tem-ple hierarchies. (In this, it was unlike some other Pagan tradi-tions, both before and after it.) Sex magic was approved of, for healing purposes, but was a voluntary matter, left to the discre-tion and choice of individuals. This was under the guidance of the older priestesses or priests, if advice was needed. My own partner in these rites, as well as in a more personal sense, was (in time, as I grew older) the priest who had been my first friend and pulled me from the sea. However, priests and priestesses did not marry.

There was no patriarchally-induced guilt about sensuality, yet emotional and psychic links were valued more than the crudely physical. Since feelings were admitted and understood much more than they are now, by both sexes, it was rare that an attraction was seen as being 'only physical', for the full range of reasons why this person and not that person was desired was more fully known. Strong attachments were formed on the basis of people being attuned to each other, psychically and emotionally, but one was expected to cultivate self-knowledge and to exercise self-discipline, to lesson sexual-emotional manipulation or trivial attachments entered into from vanity.

Children of priestly unions were reared in the temple city. Their home was called the Children's House. However, there were forms of contraception, like avoiding making love at one's fertile time, using herbal pessaries, and psychic and magical techniques to avoid conception. We used all these and they did work.

The priesthood, though romantic about love and in touch with feelings, were a lot less sentimental than most people nowadays. Whether this was true throughout society then, I do not know, but I believe that it was.

To go back to my story, but many years on, I was further up the coast now, in a northerly direction. My status had changed. I was wearing the biscuit-coloured robe over other robes and was a senior prophetess, very often working outside the temple. All the men and women who did this work had more to do with the public and were working a subtle healing magic. As the prophesies came through us, however disturbing they were, we had to transmute the pain and fear of the people to whom hard things were going to happen by also mediating a blessing of the Goddess, one that brought healing and a clear understanding of what was to come, revealing the purpose within it. We also had to give counselling on how to prepare for any forthcoming event, *without* instilling great anxiety. This was a hard job to do. As most people now would rather not know if a bad thing is about to happen to them or to someone close, it might seem as if we were hardly doing people a favour! But people then were much more fatalistic and also much more inclined to look for inner or hidden meaning in all events. So forewarning or preparation for an illness or death was not seen as so terrible. (In any case, our prophecies were as often of happiness to come. They were not always of disaster or difficulty.)

Because of the methods used, it was virtually impossible to tell someone something their innermost self didn't wish them to hear. Quite simply, their own psyches would veil it from the priesthood. And we were trained not to pry.

This was a gentle practice, requiring much skill. Platitudes were no good. One had to enter fully into an understanding of the other person's situation and all their fears. It had to be done with genuine compassion and without being glib. It was understood as being the Goddess speaking through us.

We also were expected to advise on the balance of subtle psychic factors within an individual. Similar to modern psychotherapy, but more esoterically inclined. We expressed concepts in psycho-spiritual terms, as well as psychologically. (And, in those days, the spiritual and psychological were not seen as mutually exclusive in their perspective, but simply as different dimensions of the same thing.)

Although I have not recalled it, I believe some of us were also expected to advise on matters of state - and physically to patrol Atlantis's boundaries, to keep the realm safe. Both this and the personal counselling would have been demanding work. I am sure that we must have been exhausted at times. However, we lived in a world without modern technological stresses or pollution, yet without being in want for anything. (The priesthood was supported by a system of taxation, with people giving what they could afford.) So the energy available to us would have been ample.

I remember standing on the beach, wearing black, white and red robes, with the pale, sack-coloured robe on top. I was very used to the work that I was about to do and knew that I was competent. Yet suddenly, and most unusually, I felt deep fear.

Much of what I knew that I was to speak of concerned the future of the land and people - or even of the world. For the healing magic to work best, we believed that the prophecies had to be spoken in front of other people - and then the concluding invocation for harmony and blessings had also to be given in public. However, this was not a case of giving advice or forewarning to a sovereign, but a part of the inner work of the priesthood. So this night, I was to speak in front of other priestesses and priests. And others, of course, would speak besides myself.

We were doing a rite to invoke faith, vision and hope, through the harsh times of the future.

First, we chanted an invocation and then circled together on the beach and released quantities of black birds from cages. I don't know why we did that nor what the birds were, but nowadays ravens are seen as sacred to the Dark Goddess (on the basis of Northern European folk lore and mythology) so it may have been something like that. In any case, I love the idea of releasing birds from cages rather than killing them, as a form of offering. (The practice of actually spilling another creature's blood to offer it to the deities - to whom it has always belonged in the first place - is truly an abhorrence.)

Each of us spoke to the others from a boat that was just a little way out in the water. The distance was not so great that the others could not have heard us. We were all used to this and a prowess with small boats was something we were trained in. However, unless the sea was like the proverbial millpond (which it was on this night) we often had to sit down. Sometimes, it was necessary that the others should wade out and stand around the boat.

It was soon my turn and I spoke the oracle, seeing visions of black lightning, the land breaking up, some eggs being crushed and even the Moon broken into small pieces. I explained that all this was mainly symbolic, a vision of a coming imbalance between the sexes and destruction of the feminine principle as a guiding force in society. Then I gave the blessing as I saw the new Earth arise (a new harmony between men and women), though before that I saw catastrophes, floods, explosions, all manner of human pain, incredible suffering. I felt that the new order of harmony was a long way in the future, so far off I could not measure it. And there would be many deaths and rebirths of whole cultures and great civilizations before that day. Yet here and there, in all times, the new order would show itself, among friends and lovers and small groups of people, and even sometimes among larger groups, and the hope would become rekindled and the flame of love passed on.

Then to my terror, I saw astrally that a large black bird (not a manifest one but an inner realm being) had landed upon the shoulder of the priest who was my special friend. The man whom I loved above all others and who loved me. I knew that this meant he was going to die soon. As an oracular priestess, I had no choice but to speak of it, publicly, then pronounce a blessing. I did so. Our eyes met across the water in what was really goodbye, even though I knew he would not die for a while.

I was helped ashore, very upset and shivering.

I went and sat with my friend. Characteristically, he avoided mentioning what had just happened, but put an arm round me in comfort, Later on, we would speak of it, but not during a rite.

I felt that life without him would be very lonely. I pondered the connection between love and death, deciding that separation from those we love is the saddest thing there is, even if we are certain we will be reborn and meet again. (Since then, I have learned to see it differently. Separation by death is less sad than the withering of love in those who both still live.)

Now I was in the same situation as others whom I had formerly counselled and it was a very bleak place to be - and no one yet had come to counsel me or pronounce a blessing, though I knew that would happen.

Life can seem very long. I suddenly could not see the link between love and prophecy.

Not wanting to recall the moment of my lover's death, I

moved on past it to the next important event. After some years of prophecy, I decided to perform a major act of magic, by the means of bringing an end to my own life. I would take the pain of separation, a pain which had never been healed, and I would give myself to the ocean, so that the Dark Goddess could trans-form the pain. This was far more than simple suicide, because the giving of myself to the Goddess would be preceded by much preparation and invocation and would be for a purpose. I saw it this way. I still hurt - far past the usual period of mourning - because I had not enough love and understanding within me to transcend pain. I also did not have enough vision, in a personal sense (for myself rather than for the world), to feel hope, and not enough love for others to let them fill the emptiness.

The blessings pronounced for me had not, ultimately recon-ciled me to my loss. I did not blame those who had given them nor did I see the skills we worked with as inadequate, in gener-al. Rather, I knew that no skill or technique on Earth could take the place of individual growth in understanding or strength of spirit, nor make these unnecessary. So I would sur-render completely to the Dark Goddess and then She would use my whole life force to change me, restoring vision and hope for a future life, at the moment of my death.

Moving forward again, there was darkness, the ocean and dis-tant shore lights, and the rocking of the waves under my boat. I made a last invocation that in future lives I would learn about love between man and woman, in a personal sense, and how this emotion related our instincts to the world of spirit - and how loss could be borne if the love was deep. I made an invo-cation to *understand love* and to live in and for that.

Then I gave myself to the sea.

This was my first life as a priestess of the Goddess of the Moon and Tides, a Dark Goddess whom I knew as Meri. In it, I can see quite definitely the main themes of my own spiritual direction. The worship of the Goddess as a transcendent power who is yet shown forth in nature, the taking of risks for the sake of true magic, the belief in the healing power of prophecy and words. And, as in most other past lives that I have recalled, a special relationship with a man as a focal theme. Did the piece of magic I chose to end my life with decide this theme as a major one, in many lives to come? I think that it did.

There is obviously a link here with prophecy, the link that I suddenly felt I had lost back there in Atlantis, just after I knew that my lover would soon die. The threads of fate are spun because of our desires. We also spin threads collectively, because of group desires. It must be admitted that these wishes are not always for what is best for us, for they are not based on wisdom. But still, personal desires spin our personal fate, within the context of the threads spun by many, and interwoven with them. Most personal desires are based upon our soul's seeking of understanding and fulfilment, though we do not always see how we may best gain these.

Themes repeat themselves in life after life, because we are involved with them and have desired it to be so. When such a desire has been further promoted by deliberate magic, the effect is increased and other desires become amalgamated with it, or subordinated.

Transcript of Some Guidance about Past Life Recall

Rae:　　Was what I saw of the temple of Meri from a genuine past life?

Guide:　Yes and no. You do not always see your past lives as they actually happened. You see, instead, your own memories of them. As you know from your experience in this present life, a memory can be distorted. What you remember of the past and what really happened may not be quite the same thing. This is particularly so with the events from long ago, or when they were highly charged with disturbing emotions. You really did have past lives in Atlantis but it was so long ago that the memory is blurred. Images of twentieth century Britain are sometimes superimposed on or mingled with Atlantis. But what you saw was true in essence.

The problems in accurate recall arise from your

method, the light trance. You could recall much more clearly and powerfully in deep trance. You would not be so much remembering things then as almost reliving them, exactly as they happened. But this would bring buried aspects of your psyche too quickly into full consciousness, without giving you a chance, in your present circumstances, to integrate them fully. And that could be quite dangerous for you, unless you had some assistance from someone with the right training in relevant disciplines.

With your present method, you risk inaccuracies in recall, especially when you lack concentration. But there is no risk of psychic damage. And your method, although undramatic, is usually successful. You will not recall any Atlantean life in detail. That would take a very long time to do, since any life is complex. So you remember the bold outlines of what, to you, mattered most: your personal history in love and the essence of spiritual teachings.

Trances and visions undertaken or received in a past life can be recalled more easily than mundane events. This is because you were in a different state of consciousness than the everyday, when you first experienced them. Details of ordinary life in Atlantis usually were recorded by you when in a more superficial frame of mind, unless there was a great emotional impact at the time.

There will always be some superimposition, blurring and distortion in past life recall, with your present method. Do not worry about this as the essence is genuine. The past lives were real.

For example, when the priest wrote down the name 'Meri' for you, in Atlantean script, your memory, which does not recall that lettering (especially as at the time you could not read!) filled in the gap by picturing present-day writing. You remembered the word, you remembered the sound 'Meri', and your present-day English self superimposed European lettering over the words of the old script. You will have to take this on trust. There is no proof that anyone can give you. But, by accepting it, your soul will be enriched.

4

Sea Mother of the World,
Dark Queen of the Dead

The memories I have just shared seem to be about a key life. That is, it formed my direction and gave themes for many lives to come. I think that is why I was able to recall it at some length. It was also a happy life. A time of great blossoming and so, unconsciously, I am keen to remember it. Even the final suicide did not seem, at the time, like an admission of failure. I *could* have gone on living. But I saw giving myself to the Lady of the Sea as a reasonable piece of transformative magic. Attitudes were different then from our present-day ones. If I could not make the necessary changes within myself, without giving my entire life-force to the project, then it was seen as correct to do what I did, so long as the action was voluntary. Because of my former and unbroken vows as a priestess, I had to give my life, in life after life, to this quest from the stance of a mystic, one whose vocation is religious. To a priestess of the Goddess there seemed, and seems, no difficulty in this. For we in the Goddess tradition do not see sexual or personal love as somehow unspiritual. This is because - paradox again - we recognize the presence of impersonal, transcendent powers within the experience.

To turn to another aspect of this past life memory, I have asked myself what evidence I really have for believing that Mari, whose priestess I am in this life, was at one time worshipped in Atlantis, by the name of Meri. And there is none, apart from the voice of my memory. I must confess that. The syllable Ma, or variations on it, is everywhere connected with the word mother, and not merely as slang. There are many Goddess names from around the world which begin with or contain it - a syllable like Ma or Mer, or something close to it, conveying the idea of Mother or Mother Sea. So it is rather unlikely that the Goddess was not known by this name in Atlantis, but I cannot prove it.

Here are some versions and variations I know of, Marah, Marian, Marina, Marianne, Mary, Mari, Merjan, Miriam, Moera, Myrrhine, Myrta - and these are just some! She has been worshipped in many cultures throughout the world, for many thousands of years. From India, where Hindus know her as Kau-Mari, or Kel-Mari, to Syria, where She was called Meri and worshipped with Her serpent consort Yamm, to ancient Egypt as Meri-Ra (a Goddess-God deity combining water and fire) to Iran (formerly Persia) as Merjan, to the Basque region of medieval Spain, where She was 'Mari of the Witches', to Ireland as the Morrighan (that much maligned Goddess) to Celtic Britain and also Brittany, where She was Mari-Morgan or Morgen or Morgan Le Fay or Morgaine (recognized as a Goddess long before She was demoted to the role of King Arthur's scheming sister).

Wherever She was worshipped She has been associated with magical powers, very often with prophecy. She has been linked with the Moon and Underworld or faery realm, and seen as Mother of the Spirits, by whom we are reborn. Her realm is often across water on a sacred island or is within or under or symbolized by sea. In the same vein, there are also Maya of South America, Yemaya of Brazil and Africa, the Sea Goddess, and Maya, the Indian Goddess who bestows dreams and visions.

There were priestesses and priests who foresaw the destruction of Atlantis, not long before it happened. These are traditionally supposed to have fled to lands like Egypt and other eastern or middle-eastern countries to preserve the sacred teachings. They would have taken their deities' names with them. From there, the teachings could have spread to many places.

Earlier than this, since Atlantean people travelled and would have discussed their tradition with folk of other continents for many generations before the destruction, it is likely that ideas about Meri and other Atlantean deities spread by a sharing of concepts and perhaps mutual influence. (And the name Meri could have come to Atlantis via the other lost continent, Mu, said to have been submerged beneath the Pacific.) This sharing is highly probable, in light of how some other religious ideas and Goddess names have migrated in other times.

Some writers, like Olivia Robertson and Murry Hope, believe that Dana (or Danu) was a prime Atlantean Goddess, rather than or as well as Mari. Thereafter, Her worship spread, first to India and then, by way of Scandinavia, to Ireland.

Plato's account states that the Atlantean deities were called Poseidon and 'the nymph Cleito'. (In patriarchal times, Cleito was demoted from Goddess to nymph. This often happened in tales of Goddesses, a process thoroughly documented by feminist scholars.) But Plato makes clear he is giving us Greek equivalents and not the original Atlantean names. However, I would not wish to give the impression that I believe that all worship of the Dark Goddess, as Sea-Mother, Prophetess, First Sea of Space or Queen of the Dead, originated solely in lost Atlantis. There have been many other great civilizations all over the world. Some were definitely matriarchal (the earliest ones all seem to have been so) and their views differed greatly on polarity and God-Goddess relationship from those I have described as once current in Atlantis. Others were beginning to lose the balance and fall into patriarchy, or had definitely done so. But all would have known the Dark Goddess under some name or another. It is just that my own earliest experiences of Her, or the earliest I remember, were in Atlantis, and my personal interest - and story - is based in that. In other cultures, there may or may not be Atlantean strands in Dark Goddess worship. When I find them they are to me, personally, very interesting. (So, of course, I am fascinated by the tradition that the Celtic Morgan of Brittany and Great Britain came here 'from Atlantis'.) They are also significant for the emotional and mythological impact of Atlantis as a place, regardless of any past life recollections.

I would now like to describe briefly some other depictions of the Dark Goddess, than Meri of Atlantis. Some of them may derive partly from Her and some do not. As I hope to show, all their myths are relevant to our own times, although their stories are timeless.

KALI

In India, the main name by which the Dark Goddess is known is Kali. Before I go on to say something about Her, this fiercesome Goddess with the rather disturbing reputation, I would first like to quote some words by Olivia Robertson from her book *Urania*. 'Evil is but the distorted shadow of the actual and cannot relate to eternal reality.' Elsewhere, she states that most people do not worship real deities but shadows of deities. She means that true Goddesses and Gods are always beneficent. *They* are powers which are always harmonious, like Love or Truth or Death, the great purifying force bringing rest and rebirth. They are not cruel or malicious. But most of us do not worship the true deities. Instead, we misunderstand the powers They represent - and then worship the resulting shadow deity we have created inside our own minds! Christianity offers a clear illustration of this point. For who would recognize the gentle, chaste (or self-disciplined, depending which gospel you read) but compassionate and caring Jesus, who refused to take part in stoning an adulteress, in the uptight, puritanical, intolerant killjoy, self-righteous, violently judgemental and punishing - yet also sentimental - who is worshipped by millions? Many millions of Christians, both in the past and, on the evidence of their avowed beliefs, in the present day, have preferred a shadow deity. And this dreadful false Jesus has been believed to mediate the true presence of God the Father, whose own depictions in the Old Testament do not bear too much close examination! These are shadow deities - and not the real thing.

Exactly the same problem exists with Goddesses. For both political and psychological reasons, the Dark Goddess especially has been seen as both unpredictable and violent, prone to curse enemies and to work for their destruction. Sometimes, She has continued to be worshipped, i.e. in Pagan cultures. And sometimes, i.e. in monotheistic, patriarchal cultures, She has been rejected as evil, on account of these attributes (the business of smiting enemies being seen as belonging solely to 'God the Father'). Either way, we are not looking at a real Goddess, but a shadow deity.

I have to say these things before talking about Kali because She, like many other Dark Goddesses, has a mythology which is most intimidating to modern westerners, and all too easily interpreted as simply demonic. She is a Death Goddess - She purifies and renews - and is ruler of the realm where ancestors live. But She can be wrongly perceived as the cruel bringer of the end, rather than a natural power who brings blessings. She is seen as an eerie, 'supernatural' being, one who is prone to enjoy both death and decay for their own sake - a Shadow deity and not the real thing.

Kali, even though Her symbols have frightening connotations, is a beneficent deity in terms of the pattern of all existence, as well as in our own lives. To explain this, I shall first briefly outline Her myth and then reinterpret it.

A long time ago the world, which is Kali's domain, had become corrupt and degenerate because of human evil. People did not live anymore by love and wisdom but were selfish and unthinking. They used each other and the Earth cruelly, so that there was no possibility of health or happiness. Kali was so filled with rage that She became violent. She dealt out death everywhere She went, creating huge earthquakes and mighty floods. With Her four winnowing arms and trampling feet, Her teeth bared, She brought death to entire countries. But Her consort, who is the God Siva, wanted to save a few, thinking they could become wise and loving if time was given. He laid Himself down beneath Kali's feet and so Kali trampled Her own husband to death, but some humans were spared.

Thus, Kali is portrayed as vengeful, unforgiving and violent, at least when She feels offended. In pictures, She is shown holding a severed head. Her necklace is of skulls and She carries a sword. Her colour is black. But if, for Kali, we read Gaia, the inner spirit of our Earth, She whose presence manifests in Earth's ability to protect natural balance, even if She must act ruthlessly to achieve this, then it becomes clear why She appeared in a time of great evil and did what She did. A corrupt humanity, prepared to abuse nature and break with natural justice, will always eventually invoke Kali-Gaia. If we disturb the balance of nature too far then She must appear. She has no choice. The resulting remedial action will then be violent, has been so in the past when other generations overstepped the mark, as many of the world's religious traditions, and the evidence found by unorthodox scientists, bear witness. But Her action can cleanse the Earth and restore balance.

The God Siva, who is Time, or Guardian of the Cycles of Time, shows by His action that sometimes even Time must be destroyed - or transcended? - if life is to go on. More immediately, He gives His own life, showing in Hindu form the archetypal role of god-heroes everywhere - one who sacrifices Himself for the people. (Like any other God, He is then resurrected.) To get to the crux of it, He really shows that if humanity is to survive, then Time must be given to the Dark Goddess.

At this point, in our own culture, we might still be able to invoke Her as a less violent presence than in Her myth and voluntarily to give our time to Her. She would then be inclined to sweep away our corrupt values and decadent ways, but leave us alive. This requires willingness in us, personally and collectively, to give things up (things like selfishness and greed and over-consumption). Otherwise, it may be too late and we shall lose all.

That is my reading of Kali's myth. I hope that I do not seem to be preaching or scare-mongering - but the writing is, as they say, on the wall. And anyone who has been part of Atlantean culture knows all about this, since we have been down this road before. As, no doubt, have other people from other cultures, over the vast time span of human history.

Siva's action shows how, in the passing of time, nature renews Her creatures and life goes on. We could invoke Him now, so that His passing need not be a violent catharsis, followed by a long rest between lives (a very long rest!) for most human beings, while Earth renews Herself and, perhaps, a few remaining folk start us all off again.

Siva really is about giving Time to the Dark Goddess. This

might be as simple for us as just slowing down. Our culture has an obsession with speed, with living in the fast lane. We are all supposedly saving time, but for what? Most people in the western world feel over-stretched. They feel they are always having to hurry to keep up. Surprisingly, this affects the unemployed as well as those with jobs. We all feel that we must hurtle from A to B at breakneck speed. A slower pace of life would encourage simplicity and a lot less reliance on gadgets that 'save time'. We might then have more leisure.

People from tribal cultures have commented on how little time we modern westerners really have, just to hang loose or to be creative. Their lives are more leisurely. This is not just a matter of indolence created by a warm climate. It is about lack of the kind of cultural pressures we all live with, and which fundamentally serve an exploitative, capitalistic elite. The only wealth a poor person has, the only capital, is time - unless this is stolen as under-waged labour, or diverted into consumerist pursuits. To change all this requires a deep transformation of our entire culture, both personally and also collectively. As recent history has often shown, political change (though essential) is not enough.

Giving our individual time to the Dark Goddess can also mean finding some time to spend with Her, in trance or meditation. If we honour Her deliberately like this, She may give us new visions of how life could be, if all beings were in harmony and if we lived wisely. We could then give time to realizing these dreams, in so far as we are able, in our own lives. This might mean practical things like recycling, or emotional and psychic changes in our relationships, or both. But, above all, She could work magic. There is something about turning to Her, in prayer or meditation, that can produce change in unexpected ways. Sometimes, this may be preceded by a purification, in much the same way as an illness purges the body of toxins. For instance, there may be the loss of a job which was doing no good to the worker, nor to the environment. The ways in which new health and creativity express themselves, following Her action, can be as surprising personally as they are politically and collectively.

Kali and Siva are really at one. She is often depicted squat-

ting astride Him, in sexual union. Dark Goddesses are powerfully sexual. You could say that, in this way also, She takes His
life, that life can go on. This is true for any man, in sexual congress. Don't we say that his energy is 'spent'? And that he
undergoes 'the little death' after orgasm? Yet it is by this giving
of his life-force to the Goddess, in the person of his female partner, that the continuity of life is assured.

Furthermore, the Presence of Kali can transform a man's own
life. There are some sexual unions that bring such profound
change, both inwardly and in worldly circumstances, that the
man's life is not the same again. Everything crashes around him
and his world seems to die. Later on, he enjoys a new way of
life as, almost, another person. The change is so thorough and
entire that, though he doesn't die physically, he is almost as
though reincarnated.

This is one reason why men can fear women. They sometimes mediate Kali as directly as that. Almost any man can
sense when a particular woman would do this for him. But
change, even for the better, is not always welcome. Even
though Kali does not take anything unless it is outworn or pre-
venting new creativity, human fear of the death that precedes
rebirth, the loss of a comfortably familiar life and old expectations, can make a man turn away from the woman in panic. Or
worse, to perceive her as somehow demonic.

But when such relationships are consummated, the man, as
Siva, also brings change for the woman. He gives as good as he
gets! Because he has given his time to her, in a most profound
way, she will never be quite the same again. Also, in mediating
Kali, she is acted upon by Kali, but can't experience this unless
Siva first gives her his time.

Not all sexual relationships are of the nature of a Kali-Siva
exchange that transforms both lives. Those that are may be
brief or last for a long time. And the transformation may be
short and sharp or long-lasting and recurrent. When the transformation is done, the partners may choose to part or may stay
together. Or they may remain together for some years and then
part. The pattern varies.

Kali's action is not always physically sexual, so it is also possible for great change to occur through an unconsummated rela-

tionship. This process, however, can be no less harrowing than a love affair that expresses itself in natural affection. There is also a great risk of short-changing the Goddess and so short-circuiting the transformative process, but it can be done.

In the last resort, Kali liberates all the transient in life and gives it true being in the realms of the eternal. (This is what it means to die.) Often, She achieves it through crisis or catharsis, which is why our own age of trial and tribulation is called a time of Kali. We resent this because it is frightening. But we cannot yet know what the rebirth will be like.

Metaphorically (and this can be seen in terms of burial after a physical death), Kali pushes us *down*, under, within, so that we can rise up.

A short prayer to Her could be something like this:

'Divine Goddess Kali, purifier and renewer, take from our lives all the ways in which we cause harm to ourselves and others and to the Earth. Let us live purely in love and by wisdom from now on. Transform unkindness and cruelty within us to compassion and courage. Bless all our passion for those we love, that new ways may arise and new works or new children.'

Lastly, I must add that Kali's action in transformative sexuality can be experienced in single sex relationships. Homosexual passion can bring as deep change as the heterosexual can, to ourselves and our lives. It would still remain the case that one partner would mediate Kali and the other one Siva, but, as already stated, these powers are beyond gender.

Isis

In a very different style from that of Kali, the Goddess Isis of Egypt has also a Dark side. She is not portrayed as a violent force, but is a more obvious kind of Saviour-Goddess. Yet there are statues of Her in black. She is a Dark Goddess as well as a Bright one. Often known as Isis the Enchantress, She has the secret of magical power, and this faculty alone marks Her out as of the Dark realm. She has the Dark Goddess power to bring healing by magic. The deep, blessed, creative power of the

Dark, from which Light is born.

When Her husband, the God Osiris, was killed by His broth-er Set, and the pieces of His dead body scattered far and wide, She magically restored Him to life, in the person of His son, Horus. Whereupon Osiris Himself rose to His new power as God of the Underworld and Guardian of the Mysteries. The land, which had been devastated at Osiris's death, for He had been a just king and in His reign there was peace and abun-dance, was then restored to harmony and happiness. Isis agreed to limit the power of Set from then on, but She would not have Him killed, preferring to be merciful. In this, She not only dis-played compassion, but acknowledged that creative forces in life must sometimes be balanced by the destructive if over-pro-liferation is not to destroy health (as with cancer cells).

In Her travels upon Her mission to save Osiris and resurrect Him, Isis was sometimes assisted by Nepthys, Her Dark sister and other self, whose husband was Set. They were also some-times accompanied by Anubis, who was Nepthys's son. (His father was Osiris, since Nepthys had disguised Herself as Isis to become pregnant by Him because Set was infertile.)

These are the brief outlines of the Isis myth. The actual story is longer and more complex - and there are variations upon the theme, including patriarchal ones which play down the role of the Goddess. But that is it, in essence. Isis and Osiris are represented by a twin star called Sothis. They are the eternal lovers and twin souls, forever linked in life and in death. This shows the interaction of Goddess and God, in the cycles of creation.

The story is different to that of Kali and Siva, in the way the themes are handled and attributes shared out among protago-nists. However, the underlying message is the same. We must have destructive forces as well as creative, but the destructive must not go too far. And the Goddess, by the power of Her pas-sionate involvement with life, brings renewal and transforma-tion. Where the stories differ is that Set, who is the selfish and destructive element in humanity (and motivated by jealousy), as well as being a natural power in the universe, is seen as directly responsible for creating havoc in the land. He does not bring earthquakes and floods, but His action brings suffering throughout nature. In the previous myth, by contrast, the destroyer is the Goddess, though She does not create but purifies the Wasteland. Like Kali, Isis is nature, and She is the fundamental regenerative power.

In *The Golden Ass*, a novel written by Lucius Apuleius, an initiate of the Mysteries of Isis, about 150 C.E., Isis speaks these words: 'I am Nature, the universal Mother, mistress of all the elements, primordial child of time, sovereign of all things spiritual, queen of the dead, queen also of the immortals, the single manifestation of all gods and goddesses that are . . .'

One of Her symbols is the boat and ships were dedicated to Her. Her own boat, however, was the one in which the dead sailed on their way to the realm in which they would be given rest and renewal. Her outspread wings protect all the dead and She restores them to life. That is why She is often depicted suckling a child.

These are just some of the facts about Isis. In Her worship in the past, there was sometimes corruption, as in all religions. Though it is hard to see how one could use Her story to justify any wrong doing! Most of Her devotees advocated gentleness, self-knowledge and self-discipline. Some were strict vegetarians. Her mysteries were widespread throughout the Graeco-Roman world, as well as in Egypt. Also, ancient temples to Her have been found in both Paris and London.

Of old, She was known as 'mistress of the perfect black'. And more recently, therefore, She has been associated with the Lady Alchimia, or the female spirit of the process of Alchemy, a magical-symbolic system of spiritual transformation, based on early understanding of chemical reactions. I, myself, find Her compassion for all, Her courage, and Her passion for Osiris to be quite awe-inspiring.

What is interesting, in view of patriarchal assumptions about the nature of evil, is that Isis names Herself as being all nature. So nature, in Her tradition, is compassionate, not evil. It is not that we have 'fallen' into nature, but that nature is the All, including all things spiritual. And therefore, deep within Her, there is that which restores lost balance. Nature, Herself, is primarily loving, even though She contains other forces and powers (other deities) who can bring destruction! This is a basic belief of the Goddess tradition, both in Apuleius's day and now. Nature is holy.

Isis, though She is the All, is about compassion. How we reconcile that with the other face of nature as 'red in tooth and claw' involves taking a very long view of the purpose, the transformative magic, within creation, and accepting the part played in it by Set (as Isis accepted it). At the present time, as for a long time now, Osiris lies dead and His brother, Set, rules. Isis is wandering now in the search for Her lover's body. The key to Her (and to life) is love. When we act from that, we mediate Isis and help Her to resurrect Osiris, and restore the lost balance in a new form. Or, as men, we accept Her redeeming power and are transformed and then go on to restore the Wasteland to harmony and beauty, as Horus, or work magically within the Mysteries, as Osiris-Anubis.

Though Isis is Love, She is not saccharine. There is nothing in Her of the 'good wife and mother', eternally self-sacrificing and unthreatening. Her power is earthy and magical as blood. She is passionate, not demure, expressing Herself sexually and emotionally. Black Isis rules over the menstrual pole of a woman's sexuality, the mysterious time of increased psychic faculties and honest feelings, when sex, as practitioners of Tantra have explained, can be a particularly healing experience for both partners. (Or for a woman alone, during solitary sex.) It is not a fertile time in human beings, on a physical basis, though arguably it may be a time for conception of 'spirit children', in the form of ideas, works of art etc. It may even truly create 'astral offspring', those children of a woman's psyche who can take shape in inner realms, visiting her in dreams. (This is a little understood and under-explored aspect of sexual creativity, but it links with the Dark Goddess's reputation for being the Mother of faery children as well as of younger deities.)

In animals, the period of bleeding is actually the only time of conception. In either case, whether human or animal, and with or without accompanying sexual activity, it draws us close, by the presence of blood, to the numinous and inner realms, reminding us of mortality.

Nuit, the Mother of Isis, is the Great Deep. Her body arches over the night sky. She is both Death and Birth and gives birth to the galaxies. She is the Mother of the Gods, the One from whom all life comes. Isis inherits Her Mother's attributes but, above all, it is love for which Isis is renowned. Through Her, Nuit walks on Earth and Her response is love, a love that takes Her on a quest for Her husband's dead body, to restore Him to life by the use of Her magic. Her passion for Osiris is eternal. It outlasts death and it brings resurrection. Her compassion for all, including Set, and Her breadth of vision and understanding, are Goddessly attributes that bring inspiration. Here is a prayer to Isis:

'Great Goddess Isis, you who are loving and compassionate, we call upon you to redeem us. Bring us to wisdom and joy and fullness of life. Be in our hearts that we, too, act with love and understanding. Arouse within us all love's magical power, to heal and restore.'

TIAMAT

The Babylonian Goddess Tiamat was known as the Sea-Mother. She was understood to be the primordial ocean from which all life came, not just Earth life but Earth Herself and the entire universe. This ocean symbolized a state in which there was 'no thing', and yet which actually held the potential for all things. It was felt to be both a spiritual image of creative power and also manifest upon Earth as the great oceans. Tiamat was the ruler of the tides, both the inner and outer. She not only was the principle of nature's rhythms, She also ordained fate. Therefore, all the ebb and flow of fortune were in Her hands. Sadly, the myth that we now have about Tiamat is a patriarchal version. It is told in full in 'The Epic of Creation' from the Enuma Elish, and here are the main themes.

Tiamat, the Sea Goddess, and her twin Apsu, the God of Freshwater Seas, were the first Mother and Father of all life. By them were created the stars, all the signs of the zodiac and the fair Earth. This happened because Tiamat gave birth to two other deities, who were also twins, one male and one female. These in their turn conceived another pair, who gave birth to Ea and Anu, or Earth and Sky. From these last two were descended the many minor deities, one of whom created humanity.

The younger gods disturbed the eternal peace of Tiamat and Apsu and therefore Apsu complained of their unruliness to Tiamat. He even suggested destroying them, since their actions were causing Him pain. Tiamat agreed that the actions of the younger gods were unpleasant, yet refused to destroy that which She and Apsu had created.

Then the leader of the Annunaki, who were the younger gods, killed Apsu. Tiamat's sorrow was immense and She decided that, after all, She would fight the young gods. She gave birth to or 'caused there to be' many 'monsters' to fight for Her, such as dragons and fish men. At first, the Annunaki expected defeat. But Marduk, a hero who was later to be named a Sun God, led them into battle and they gained victory over Tiamat and Her forces. Since they could not completely destroy Her, they cut Her in half and stretched one piece of Her body across the Earth and the other over the sky. In later tales She was known as a mere sea-monster, no longer the All-Mother.

On one level, this story is about the take-over, by men and institutions of patriarchal spirituality, from an earlier matriarchal and Goddess-worshipping culture, a process described at length by Starhawk in her book *Truth or Dare*. But behind the story about a political power struggle between men and women is another story about the cycles of creation. Tiamat, as the Mother of Life, created all beings, together with Her twin, the All-Father. She therefore, began all the processes of fate. Apsu, the Father, was in accord with Her and Their harmony and peace were eternal. They, together, were the Source. But Their children, who were the separate powers and beings in creation, were necessarily distant from Them, and so had parted from the original wisdom. That is why they became 'noisy' and 'hurtful'.

The All-Father, foreseeing trouble ahead, began to have doubts at this point. The children had left behind the true peace of the innermost spirit realm (the peace of the Mother's womb) and were engaged in the violent, sometimes harrowing, processes of life. There was suffering and conflict and competition. This disturbed Apsu. The children finally turned on their own creators, the Mother and Father, and killed the Father. In other words, the harmonious Apsu, Guardian of Divine Law, who was at one with the Mother, was destroyed by a new form of masculine energy as time went on. The masculine and the feminine fell into conflict. Tiamat decided, belatedly, to fight them. Or, in a less patriarchal understanding of the tale, once we have murdered our concept of nature's laws (Apsu) and turned our back on love (the Mother Goddess Tiamat) we have to deal, with what seem like the harsh blows of fate - or nature's disturbance. In reality, like the Sun God Marduk, we brought this on ourselves. Tiamat tried to defeat the belligerent forces of patriarchy, and perhaps this at least limited their power. As the end of the tale shows, they could not destroy Her. To put it another way, the Deep Feminine aspect of the universe (an essence beyond gender) struggled to stop an unbalanced masculine power from taking over, once the true eternal Masculine had been 'destroyed'. That the Masculine should be so sacrificed was inevitable, because manifestation of life, the creation of the universe, meant separation from the Ground of All Being (the Goddess) and fragmentation of wisdom and a 'fall' into unwisdom, violence and pain. This would always be so, until, in the cycles of time, the true Masculine (a principle of harmony and observance of nature's laws) could be reborn.

But if the Great Mother Tiamat is to give rebirth to Apsu, Her own sundered body must first be reunited. In the world of humanity, we may see this sundering of the body of the Feminine as the splitting of woman, in the patriarchal mind, into an earthy whore or 'unearthly' madonna. Into the 'filthy' and pornographic body of the sexual woman, full (as the Church Fathers used to complain) of 'carnal lusts', or into a sexlessly 'spiritual' being without self-assertion or sensuality. A beautiful, obedient virgin who hardly has a body and then becomes (without carnal enjoyment, of course) a self-sacrificing mother figure.

The myth recounts that Marduk 'made' humanity, out of the blood of the slain consort of Tiamat, sometimes called Kingu. It certainly sounds as though he has made human culture, as we know it now!

What we can do about this begins inside ourselves, with our personal and individual decisions. If we reject the so-called separation between our spirituality and our bodies (in particular, the sexuality of our bodies) and celebrate physicality for what it is, a manifestation of Divine principles, we can begin to reunite the sundered body of Tiamat. This means reclaiming our sexuality as sacred and vibrantly beautiful, whether we wish to express that on our own, or with a partner. (And whether or not we are heterosexual.) One simple way to begin this resolving of duality is to take off your clothes in order to say your prayers. To stand not ashamedly but proudly naked. This is a rite of Tiamat.

First, make fresh and clean the most peaceful, comfortable room in your home. Put flowers or green leaves (or dried fruit and berries in winter) round the room in preparation. Set up a small table or other clean wooden or stone surface, as an altar, and have upon it two candles and a bowl of water. Draw the curtains and light the candles and take off everything you are wearing. Now, standing before the altar, pray to the Mother Goddess - and the All-Father also, if you would like to - giving thanks for the beauty of nature, including your own. You can do this no matter what age you are, and even if you do not think you are the perfect physical specimen (Who does think that!) Thanks can be given for the beauty with which all your physical processes co-ordinate. All on its own, your heart beats and supports life. Your limbs can lift and run or dance. Your breasts can nourish babies, or perhaps have already done so. Your mouth can speak, your whole body can make love, your vulva and womb can give pleasure and life. (Even those with marked disabilities can celebrate like this, for where there remains *life* there is always some physical beauty. My own disability is that my pelvis is narrow and thus I cannot give birth without caesarean section. As a result, I am scarred, in more ways than one. I must, therefore, celebrate the beauty I *do* have. I fully realize I am actually fortunate. This is not such a hard track to walk, in my own case.)

The rite is not solely for woman. Men can do it as well and, in fact, it is as important that they should. The list of their reasons to give thanks would, of course, differ in some respects from women's lists, but they have as many of their own.

It is best to begin by celebrating and giving thanks for the whole beauty of creation, mentioning all that has moved you - the trees, hills, landscapes, the moods of the sea, all plant life, animals, and your own animal self, in glowing detail.

This celebration of self is the opposite of narcissism, since you are associating yourself, through it, with all creation, and the deities who made you. If you can work the rite with a lover, celebrating each other with compliments and caresses, after prayers to the Goddess, so much the better. You can, if you wish, conclude by making love. Afterwards, say, 'May I live, by the Mother's will, in perfect harmony of spirit and body.' Annoint yourself on the forehead with water from the bowl Extinguish the candles before you dress.

If the idea of saying your serious prayers in the nude really makes you feel embarrassed, that only goes to show how far the body of the Goddess has been split within human minds.

Tiamat is in the eternal realms, as well as in this transient world. She is eternity. In that dimension, Her body has never been cut in half. There, She is simply the Mother, entire love. She is a true Dark Goddess, Mother of the Otherworld, from which this mortal world comes into being. She rules the tides of all fate and so can bestow vision and prophetic skills.

Some scholars believe that the war described in the Enuma Elish may have been based on actual physical battles for supremacy between the matriarchal Goddess-worshipping people of southern Sumeria and the expanding patriarchal civilization further to the north. This is probably true. But those battles were fought many years ago. Before we can turn the tide now, against patriarchy, we must look beyond violence to the reuniting of ourselves, body and spirit at one. We must first heal the old wound of sundering we have internalized. Then our world, also, may be at one.

Patriarchal Babylonians celebrated the defeat of the 'sea

monster' Tiamat, by Marduk, each year. She was now to be assigned 'shadow' qualities - chaotic violence, ugliness and malice. From Her dismemberment a new world was made, one of authoritarianism and hierarchies, exploitation and suffering, oppression of the poor, denigration of women and down-grading of their status in spiritual terms, as well as politically. Humankind out of harmony with itself and, increasingly, with all other beings. This is a world we are all horribly familiar with - because we live in it.

Prayer to Tiamat:

'Divine Goddess Tiamat, the giver of fate, help us to be in harmony with all the changing phases of the cycles of creation. Help us to understand them and live with wisdom. May we also perceive our own destinies and be at one with them. You are within us, in womb and heart. We can see your realm also in the darkness and deep, when we look up at the night sky or visit the ocean. By your love and power, may we keep our own balance in life's shifting tides. We thank you for the joy of our own living bodies, the expression of our spirits.'

PERSEPHONE AND HECATE
From the Homeric hymn to Demeter comes a story of a Dark Goddess very differently portrayed from Tiamat. Persephone is both the Queen of the Dead and also Daughter of the Goddess of Abundance, who was called Demeter by the Greeks. Demeter can be seen as a three-in-one Goddess, a Triple Mother, as indeed She is. Her other two aspects are Her own daughter Persephone and the Crone Goddess, Hecate. This gives us the usual Maid, Mother and Wisewoman Goddess. However, Persephone is both the younger face of the Dark Goddess Hecate and the Daughter of the Bright Goddess.

Demeter, as the Bright Goddess, makes crops grow and the land fertile, while Hecate's realm is the night and winter, dark caves and all psychic experience. That the year must return to the dark winter season, when all vitality sinks into the Earth and life turns inward, is one very obvious level of interpretation of the story of Persephone. In springtime, She comes back from the spirit realm to rejoin Demeter,

Hecate, with Her moonlight lamp, shines in the passages between life and death. She is the way-shower who helps with Her wise magic. The realm of the Dead belongs to Her, as much as to Hades/Pluto.

I hope the above shows how the Dark and Bright Goddesses are actually one, with the Dark Maiden, who is also the Daughter of the Bright One, uniting them in the ebb and flow of all creation.

(Needless to say, this understanding of Hecate/Persephone is quite unlike that shown in the Chaldean oracles, the patriarchal system of Neo-Platonic theurgy, in which She is depicted as World Soul, and associated with both the Moon and Death, but not as the great creative power of Inner Realms in Her own right, merely as a representative of the Father. She is seen as an emanation of the Mother - who in this system is 'below' the Father - and Her function is to give shape to the Father's thoughts!)

The story will already be familiar to most, but here it is in essence. One day, Persephone was out walking, alone, in the beautiful fields and woodlands of spring. She bent down and picked a narcissus, admiring the scent and colour. But this seemingly small deed caused the earth to spring open, right there at Her feet. Then Hades, the Lord of the Dead, came out through the crack from the Underworld and He abducted Her. He took Her away to His realm within Earth, where the spirits of the dead live. (This place is elsewhere described as being encircled by an underground river. To get there, or back, one must 'pay the ferryman'. The Dark Goddess's queendom is most often in or across water.)

Demeter was desolate at the loss of Her daughter. She became worn and haggard in Her search for Persephone. In the course of Her long travels there was a time when She lived in the palace of Queen Metaneira, as a children's nurse. She tried to make Her charge, the young prince, immortal. Meanwhile, the Goddess Hecate had heard and seen the abduction of Persephone. She informed Demeter. They went together to

Zeus, the God who rules the Gods, and He told Them that He had chosen Persephone for the wife of Hades.

Demeter's outrage at this statement caused Her to halt the seasons completely. No summer came during that long year. The people prayed desperate prayers and so Zeus decreed that Persephone should return from Hades and stay with Her Mother, so long as She had not eaten any food of the dead while She was with Him. In fact, He had given Her a pomegranate, of which She had eaten some. So for only half of the year - the bright half, in summer - Persephone could return to Demeter and live in the Upperworld. For the dark half, winter, She must return to the Underworld and Hades, and reign there as queen. Hecate accompanied Her from that time on, and Demeter restored the Earth's seasons and fruitfulness returned.

The Mysteries of Demeter and Persephone/Hecate were much celebrated in ancient Greece. To the temple at Eleusis came many initiates. However, the rites they performed, though based on the above story, were kept secret. No one knows what they were, but it was reported that they brought about joyousness. It was also said that one would be happy in the Afterlife, because of them, far happier than those who had not been initiated. (This fact was noted by the Greek writer Sophocles.) It may be supposed that initiates gained a communion with Persephone/Hecate and also experienced in meditation, a joyful return with Persephone to the living and Bright Demeter. So the rites were probably of Death and Rebirth, in symbolic form.

Once again, the version we have of this story contains patriarchal elements. Zeus, the Father God, is 'in charge' and He makes the rules. Demeter can only really appeal to Him or rebel against Him. Persephone marries a God who has first abducted Her. But looking beyond all the political and social implications of this later-day version, we may see in the dual figure of Persephone/Hecate a powerful depiction of the Dark Goddess. She is both Maiden and Crone. Her skills are magical. She can happily come and go between this world and the Realm of the Dead but She rules in the spirit realm. Within

the Underworld, She prepares a 'beauty ointment' that transforms the one who uses it, as the related story of Psyche and
Eros indicates, after Psyche's visit to the Underworld.

Hecate was much worshipped as the Witches' Queen.
People have often cast spells in Her name, for She confers
magic and wisdom. Her protection was also invoked for trav-
ellers. Shrines were made for Her by roadsides, especially at
cross-roads, because She was way-shower in this world and
guide in the inner passageways between worlds. Associated
with the Moon, She was Triple Goddess in Her own right, but
of the Underworld and night, rather than of fertility.

It was Hecate who helped Demeter to find Persephone.
And, as Caitlin Mathews points out in her book *The Elements of
the Goddess*, both Demeter and Persephone take on Hecate's
appearance, for a while anyway, becoming either more haggard
or more darkly robed and pale-skinned.

As for the role of Hades, I prefer to believe that in an earlier
version He courted Persephone. Or perhaps even that She had
gone in search of Him, as Her voluntary picking of the flower
might well suggest. To say that His action gave the Dark
Goddess the right to be queen of the dead is ludicrous. As
Hecate, Her older self, She was that already. Also, the Dark
Goddess and Her partner are twin powers. They are not of the
brutal-older-man-and-yielding-young-maiden model. Balanced
between the Wisewoman and the Maiden, He must be seen as
mature. But to depict the Dark Lord of the spirit realms as a
violent abductor or even (as the story seems to imply) a possible rapist, is an outrage. (However, in patriarchal terms, such
behaviour was seen not as incongruous for a God, at this point
in Greek history, but merely as a foible or 'amorous adventure'.)

In the end, Persephone's story teaches that magical power,
both to heal and transform, is gained from the spirit realm and
won by descent into darkness, some kind of death. There, we
lose all our bearings and our former way of life. These descents
can happen to us, in our own lives, in a personal manner.
Suddenly, we fall in love or embrace a new concept, to lose the
life we had known and live in a new way. For Persephone, what
prompted this was Her picking of a narcissus. Why did She
want to do that? A narcissus is a kind of daffodil and one of its

main magical associations is love. So Persephone picked a spring flower of love and therefore invoked Hades. The message here is that if we want to experience love, we must first understand mortality, and/or that love is always a transformative force. Since the narcissus is a spring flower, the promise of rebirth is given right at the beginning, before the descent into the dark passageways.

Prayer to Persephone:

'Mysterious Goddess Persephone, Queen of the Dead, we call upon you to bless us in life and death. Annoint us with the oil that you make that gives beauty of the soul, for we know that it is blended with wisdom and love. Let us, like Psyche of old, convey your gift to the Upperworld, so that all our relationships are blessed with beauty and so made sacred.'

MORGAN/THE MORRIGHAN

The mythology of Morgan Le Fay, in Britain, now largely concerns Her life as the half-sister of King Arthur. She was reputedly malicious and destructive, Her skill in witchcraft employed to cause mischief and to further Her unpleasant schemes.

In a world where most other women were supposed to be submissive and sweetly pious, there is something about Morgan that is appealingly nose-thumbing, Despite Her supposed wickedness, it is very hard for women to dislike Morgan Le Fay. Every rebellious woman secretly admires Her - a vamp dressed in black velvet, or wearing purple and gold like a storm cloud and riding a black snake. Who wants to be pale lily-like Guinevere after that? But underneath the distortion of both feminine aspects (Morgan and Guinevere as Dark Goddesss and Bright Goddess of Arthurian tradition) there is concealed an important truth. Morgan was not, at first, seen as evil (any more than Guinevere was originally a wan, hypocritical adultress). In the first recorded account of Morgan's attributes, given by Geoffrey of Monmouth in his 'Vita Merlina', She is described as living with Her eight sisters in a realm far across the sea - an Otherworldly island - and is a healer whose skills are second to none. She can also change shape and fly through the air to wherever She wants, and is learned and beautiful. After the Battle of Camlan, She receives the fatally wounded Arthur and promises to heal him.

There is no mention here of malice or emnity. However, the later texts (especially Malory's *Morte d'Arthur*) describe bitter conflict between Morgan and the king. As shown in the popular novel *Mists of Avalon* by Marian Bradley, it is possible to interpret this as a theme based on priestesses defending the ancient faith of the Goddess against a male sovereign championing Christianity. In my belief, there may have been a priestess of Avalon (the island sanctuary of the Goddess Morgan) who fought hard against Christian displacement of the old Pagan faith. This priestess may have been known as Morgan, in much the same way that nuns are called Mary - as a sign of vocation. She may or may not have been half-sister to the king. She may or may not have existed historically as an individual person, for her tale may symbolize feelings and political actions of a great many women. But the mythology of Morgan may contain this strand, as well as those of Goddessly beauty and wisdom and healing power - the heroine-tales of a priestess or priestesses defending the old beliefs and the right to Goddess-worship.

It has also been suggested by many writers, notably Caitlin and John Mathews, who have written extensively about the Arthurian tradition, that Her actions of apparent malice show the Goddess as a moral tester, one who sets traps for unwary initiates to see if they can then sustain their integrity. This should not be perceived as the plan of a stern, judgemental deity, standing apart from creation and testing Her creatures. It is simply a symbol of what life and fate can do to well-meaning people. It says good intentions are not enough. But Morgan - the Goddess - rewards those who have learned inner strength.

Many people might nowadays doubt that Morgan is actually a Goddess, rather than simply a legendary priestess or a mythical faery-woman. However, as Gerald of Wales distastefully records, the British did definitely consider Her to be one. That She is a Dark Goddess is shown by Her rulership of the Isle of Apples, synonymous with the Celtic Land of the Dead. (And one of the many variations of Her name is, in fact, Morgue.)

The apple, 'the fruit of death which brings life', as tradition and the modern practice of Wicca both aver, indicates Morgan's gift of rebirth for all those She receives in Her island paradise. Her connection with the raven as Her totem bird (and that of Her son Owain) shows Morgan as Goddess of the aspect of nature which breaks down dead flesh, returning it to the elements and reprocessing it into other life forms. This is another function of the Goddess of Death - not only to receive the tired and wounded spirit and heal and give it rebirth, but also to deal with the dead body, so that it lives again in other creatures as nourishment. The raven, a carrion bird, symbolizes all this.

And the raven is linked in folklore and mythology with prophecy, the Otherworldly skill of foretelling the future, based on spirit messages.

Caitlin Mathews explains, in her book *Arthur and the Sovereignty of Britain*, that the Welsh, Breton and West of England Morgen or Morgan, as well as the Irish Morrighan, all seem to derive from a common source, one aspect of the Mother Goddess appearing in all traditions and functioning as both the healer and Inner Realm partner of dead heroes.

Like Morgan, the Morrighan has been depicted as a power of evil, unremittingly opposed to the hero Cuchulain, who spurns Her love and thus wins Her aggression. Olivia Robertson, in the liturgy of the Fellowship of Isis, reveals a profound interpretation, calling the Morrighan the Goddess of the unconscious realm of our deep instincts. We should befriend our instincts, in a disciplined manner, then our instincts will be our allies. To repress or deny them can lead to imbalance or violent compensation. In other words, to spurn the Morrighan's demonstrations is unwise. If we do not love our instincts, they turn against us. However, in the Fellowship's Rite of the Morrighan and Mars, She is not described as instinct alone, but as 'the hidden powers within the soul'. She is a three-fold Goddess, Maiden, Queen and Crone (Badb, Macha and Nemain). As Maiden, She can be the dark Washer at the Ford, a figure in Celtic mythology who comes not to bring death but to warn a warrior of its approach. Prophecy in all its manifestations is Her gift (and belongs also to Macha and, especially, to Nemain, the Enchantress). Her oracle states in Olivia Robertson's *Magic of Mars and the Morrighan*, a rite included in the book *Urania*, 'Knowledge of my secret of sudden death brings immortality'.

The Morrighan has been misrepresented as a war Goddess, as though She enjoyed war. In truth, Her ravens clear away the remains of any bodies left on a battlefield. It would also be true to say that much of the violence and war-mongering of mankind is a result of our lack of understanding about our own instincts. (Amongst animals, who live from instinct, the males often fight each other for a mate or for territory, but seldom to the death. And they never make war. We ourselves could do better in the intelligent fulfilling of our own instincts than the turning of human libido to the slaughtering of millions.) A new worship of the Morrighan, as Goddess of healthy instincts channelled wisely, could do away altogether with Her battle-field appearances. To imply that the Morrighan glorifies in or is patroness of war is a slander on Her name.

The raven of the Morrighan - and of Morgan - shows how all birds are connected with the Realm of the Dead (or 'bird-spirit-land'). This was graphically illustrated to me, just recently, while my partner was hand-rearing a baby blackbird, one that had been brought to him by local children. She ate huge worms, chopped into small pieces, and nothing else would do. Her eating habits showed how well she served the Dark Goddess. For worms do eat of the buried dead and of corpses in the undergrowth. And then birds eat worms, those underworld beings from the dark and moist depths. Birds, therefore, transmute the dead to an ariel-winged creature. Their action, as an image of the Queen of the Dead's way of dealing with both a body and a soul, is quite matchless.

Morgan appears in other European mythologies than the British and is mentioned by writers in Germany, Italy and France. In Brittany, She is said to have a midwife aspect and protects women in childbirth. She is also the mother of Auberon, a faery king. Water faeries in Brittany have been called mari-morgans.

In Britain, the door to Her island elysium is physically located at Glastonbury, the sacred Otherworldly island said to be a kind of inner counterpart to the famous Tor and its surrounding area. This is interesting, as Glastonbury could become again literally islanded, if the sea-defences twenty miles off at Bridgwater Bay should be broken through. In the past, as archaeology has shown, the place was a reedy, swamp-skirted island, inhabited by the 'lake people', who punted from Avalon to other bits of high ground. Mysterious to this day, a Glastonbury surrounded by sea and salt marsh must have seemed like an obvious portal between worlds.

In her book *The Ancient Secret*, the writer Flavia Anderson refers to Morgan as 'none other than the mermaid Goddess with Her mirror and cauldron'. She links Her with Atargatis, Derceto, Aphrodite and Isis. And she also describes how old rites at Glastonbury may have been (on the evidence of tradition) to do with the blending of cosmic waters with cosmic fire, or a celebration of this: Morgan, as Dark Goddess of the Waters, in union with the Fire God, by whatever name. A love by which the rainbow colours of all creation are given form.

Prayer to Morgan:

'Dark Goddess Morgan of the Sacred Island, where the dead are given rest and made ready for rebirth, we ask you to give new life to our dreams. Restore, we pray, our vision of the Earth, that we see the potential again for healing and happiness, for all. Let the people transcend aggression and find peace. Let the rule of tyrannical and greedy spirits soon cease. Let a new order prevail, a new world come to birth, by your visionary magic.'

THE BLACK VIRGIN/MARY MAGDALENE
There is also a Dark Goddess tradition within Christianity. It is not, of course, found in the orthodox faith, but in an alternative version. Statues of a 'Black Virgin' are to be found in many churches and also priories. These are mainly in France but in other countries, too. Priests can usually give no explanation, in conventional terms, for the existence of these statues, except to say that Mary lived in a hot country, so her skin was dark and thus the statues are black. But Jesus and the disciples lived in

the very same hot country and there are no black statues of *them*. Another suggestion is that these Black Madonnas are stained with an ancient grime. Once again, other statues are not so afflicted.

The Black Virgins (as they are known) are said to be exceptionally healing and wonder-working. In other words, they are magical. It is likely that some of them may have originally been images of Isis, or derived from Her or other Pagan Goddesses. But they certainly now represent an esoteric concept of the Christian Mary. This takes its main authentication from Gnostic scriptures in the minds of the literate, but makes a straight appeal, visually, to a non-scholarly folk-mystical perception of Mary as inheritor of the attributes of the Pagan Dark Goddess, as well as of the Bright Mother. As explained by Ean Begg in his book *The Cult of the Black Virgin*, these images are 'numerous in areas where paganism lingered or where the Cathars flourished'. This is because they represent an honouring of the feminine principle at variance with Catholic teachings. Black Virgins show the Virgin Mary or, alternatively, Mary Magdalene, as avatar or incarnation of the dark Goddess. Worship of Her derives from a combination of Gnostic respect for the Mother as Source of Wisdom and Pagan mystery teachings about sacred sensuality and healing power. In other words, they show a non-patriarchal image of Mary very different from that we now know as the orthodox presentation.

Cathars (those medieval practitioners of a type of Gnosticism) admitted women to the priesthood on equal terms with men. They also differed from conventional Christians in their belief that the manifest world was a place of strong evil in which we should not, actually, 'go forth and multiply' but abstain, in so far as possible, from entrapping more spirits in incarnation. This is, of course, a very deep split from traditional Pagan reverence for nature and nature spirits, as well as from Christian teachings about the world as 'fallen' but still God's good creation. Yet the Cathars idealized sexual love, and in so doing gave women as well as men a sexual freedom and autonomy otherwise unknown at that time in Christendom. They deemed that sexual love could be a true rite of the soul, a deep spiritual sacrament, refining the consciousness. This was especially so if the love was unconsummated, but could also be so if it was allowed its natural course. (Their Gnostic forebears would have disagreed about unconsummated love. They went much further and held that group sexual rites were a holy communion, in some sects, anyway.) The Cathars did not equate woman with snare-for-the-righteous or temptress or demon, for they worshipped a feminine deity, as well as a male one. They believed in a pure Spirit of Wisdom, the saviour-deity Sophia, or Holy Spirit, whose daughter (of whom Mary Magdalene would be seen as a type) was fallen into degradation in the coils of matter. The Holy Spirit was the transcendent one whose gentle touch could transform all into good and heal all wounds, if we would call upon Her. They believed this Earth to be not Her creation nor that of the true Masculine, but the work of a demiurge (the god of the Old Testament), who had borrowed from Her the essential life-power and beauty and strength with which to make a world, but whose nature was ignorance. 'Think,' said the Cathars, 'how the wild bird shrieks when the fox bites its neck in half. Every small copse contains suffering. And if life feeds upon life then that means a world in which the fox, in its own turn, lies bleeding and in pain. Nature is rife, through and through, with unconscious - and conscious - cruelty. This is surely the work of a bad god.'

All Gnostics believed in redemption of the fallen spirit of goodness in matter. Sophia was seen as the Mother of Christ, whose work was to redeem, thus the Virgin Mary was perceived as Sophia the unfallen in mortal body. She was a manifestation of the Holy Spirit. Cathars believed She would come again to transform many souls and that the life of Jesus was preparation for this. The Holy Spirit would descend in a subtle form and cause many men and women to mediate Her.

Like the Knights Templars, with whom they had contact, the Cathars believed themselves to be guardians of the Holy Grail, that numinous vessel containing the liquid that restored the Wasteland, and brought rebirth. For heretical Christians, this Cup has been identified with the womb of Mary Magdalene, or seen as symbolic of that. Women, and the Deep Feminine, were held in high esteem.

There was connection between the Cathar movement and

the troubadours, whose songs and poems were about love as a spiritual experience and woman as the mediator of a transcendent power that was good and holy, as opposed to the evil of the male demiurge.

This outright projection of all evil onto a masculine principle seems as unbalanced as the patriarchal attitude of blaming the feminine for all problems. What we need is a world where all beings are honoured and both genders are valued. The Cathars, however, were not blaming maleness as such, but a distorted masculinity too far from the Source to have maintained wisdom. In this, they were not so very far from the idea, expressed by some modern feminist writers, that the Earth, a potentially good place, is now in the grip of a possessing patriarchal entity whose influence affects nature, as well as human nature. (This entity is not identified with a real God or true Masculine principle.) Where it came from is open to question but it is my own belief that, if such a thing exists, it is created by humans, as a result of our distance from the Source and from true wisdom. We continually created this and now it possesses us. We nourish it with our own ignorance and fear and prejudices and intolerance, and now it is so large that it rules most of the world. At the very least, this dreadful psychic emanation has possessed or threatened our human consciousness for many thousands of years, affecting our world view and relationships with nature. It may also, conceivably, have distorted nature, creating a psychic atmosphere conducive to violence and predatory living. We now call this psychic essence 'patriarchy' because, in truth, the oppression of women is one of its main joys, along with all suppression of the feminine principle. But it would not be true to say it is gender specific. Unhappily, it can be mediated by women, too. Its true name may be fascism.

Judaeo-Christian Gnostics were sometimes caught by their highly structured view of the Inner Realms as a series of 'planes' and 'emanations' needing careful navigation, into concern with ritual magic of a dubious worth (an obsession with 'words of power' and so forth, known only to the elite). Cathars do not seem to have strayed into this hierarchical impasse, but some of their spiritual ancestors had great fun with it! However, the best of Gnostic teachings were concerned with a rebalancing of the sexes. For this reason, they favoured scriptures like 'The Gospel of Mary', which implied a sexual relationship between Jesus and Mary Magdalene. Making love was believed to be a ritual that, if undertaken with love and not merely as a physical release, helped to restore the androgynous inner nature of each lover, the divine integration they asserted to have been the original state of each spirit, before incarnation. The inner marriage was invoked by an outer union, as a means to psychic and psychological wholeness. Like Pagans, they knew that a trance-like state of communion with a deity could be reached through sexual activity, and that this was a deeply healing experience. Although the natural world had been made by a bad god, they honoured the soul-fire of the stars within each creature, an essence transcending both cruelty and ignorance and awakened by love. It was this that partook of true wisdom and communed with the Holy Spirit. To restore the lost unity of each being with the Spirit (achievable by love) was to begin to transform the whole world.

Though in love the soul essence communed with both the beloved and the Holy Spirit, to great healing effect, at death it was released. Mary Magdalene's role at the death of Jesus - her presence at his tomb and announcement of resurrection - can be seen as a manifestation of the Dark Goddess's power as Queen of the Dead. The tradition of the three Maries mourning at the foot of the cross has the same implication. Here we are dealing with the passage to rebirth through death and descent, and this is the Dark Goddess's own domain, as much as the psychic aspects of sexuality are Hers. Without Her, this theme could not ring true in the gospels. The release of the soul-essence at death was seen to prepare it for a new life, and though conventional Christianity portrays Jesus as having 'conquered' death, it is more true to say that death 'conquered' or transformed his transience and his suffering. The resurrection can be seen, mythically, as an indication of how, when one is prepared for death wisely (as Jesus could be seen to have been prepared by Mary Magdalene), we are transmuted by the Dark Goddess into a state of being in unity with the Source. *Then* we are no longer in ignorance.

The Black Virgin suggests many enigmatic ideas and inspires

visions. One of these is of the possible reconciliation between the Goddess traditions of the ancient world and an heretical Christianity. Whether we see Her as Mary of Nazareth or Mary Magdalene, She is Sophia and Isis by another name, the Feminine principle of wisdom in nature, and Creator Spirit. (Sophia is said to have been the originator of the worlds - until, that is, the demiurge made this one.) The Gospel of Mary indicates that Mary Magdalene was still in touch with Jesus after his death, through visionary and inner experiences. Like Isis and Osiris they were indivisible and their work was redemption. Mary Magdalene's child was said to have been fathered by Jesus, in heretical tradition.

Prayer to the Black Madonna:

'Mary of Earth, Sky and Underworld, we call upon you, black brightness of the hidden wisdom. By your guidance, we come to know love and see divinity in all beings - the buried essence of goodness. We call upon you to heal pain, to help us transcend ignorance and to bring change. Bring us to wholeness within ourselves, freedom and health. Bring our world to love.'

5

The Last Days

And when so many have worshipped a Dark Goddess, why do we now worship only the light? Why do we equate goodness with light and evil with darkness? Seeds sprout in the dark and babies first grow in the darkness of the mother's womb. Pull them out into the light, before they've grown enough, and they soon die. We need darkness to live. Too much light can be the blinding flame of many nuclear explosions. Or the shrivelling up by the Sun of all planetary life. Or the death of the magic of art that results from too much analysis, an over-illumination. As the Taoists said, any extreme becomes its own opposite, in the end. Too much light means a great darkness, whereas in deep darkness the light is born. Darkness is the rich inner realm of dream, meditation and spirit-land.

It is as though we need death in order to live. For we reconnect there, in the realm between lives, with the Mother of All, in Her transcendent, miraculous, holy and wise being. In the place where all opposites are reconciled, we are restored by Her to youth and strength, so we may be reborn, to work again at the task of helping to bring love and wisdom into full sensate being. Many are the names by which the Dark Goddess is known, from all around the world. She inspires fear, for we fear to die and fear the death of all those we love. Even though death is no final end, it still means separation for a while, and therefore, we grieve. But death sanctifies life. And so the Dark

Goddess is more than the ruler of death's realm. She is also passionate love and joyfulness and poetry.

In the foregoing chapter I have named only a few Dark Goddesses from among many, and I have given only one interpretation of Their myths and qualities. In reality, all the Dark Goddesses, including those I have not named, are one. Variations in Their mythology are due to cultural differences in times and places that are far apart, for the deities are always seen through the lens of our human limitations and cultural bias. Their attributes are too profound to be summed up, in any case. Only poetry will really do to talk about a deity, because it is enigmatic. Poetry, or a poetic reading of an old story.

The particular choices involved in my selection of Dark Goddess names imply no cultural prejudice, but a lack of knowledge and space. She will be found in all religions, from any time or place, if we look to the esoteric traditions. But if no name you know of feels right to you, you can call upon Her as 'Dark Goddess of the First Sea of Space' or 'Mother of Dreams' or by any other appropriate title. Names are much less important than the *direction* of your thought.

I want now to continue with my own story - the thread of my calling as a priestess of the Dark Goddess and how I lost touch with it for a while.

Account of a Past Life Near the Last Days of Atlantis

I was in an alcove off a blue marbled corridor, dressed in a gold robe and a headdress. I was accompanied only by a woman who had helped me to arrange my robes. We went down the corridor and then outside, into the blazing sunshine. There was a big, black rectangular building, technologically sophisticated with pipes and things on the outside, but no windows. It was used to convert solar power, but it was dangerous. It was not environmentally good like solar panels. A kind of harsh side of the Sun. This was in a part of Atlantis that was sub-tropical. I was an Atlantean but had come from a much cooler part of the continent to serve in a Sun temple.

Beside the towering building was a large, oblong, sandy pit (like a sort of sunken games field, in appearance). There were no people.

Three days later I stood there again, alone, looking at the building in some resentment. It was burned out but still smouldering. A rocket had been fired from it, though I can't recall how or why. It had something to do with the use of crystals to convert Sun energy that could be harnessed. I knew that in the intervening three days, I had been asked to bless something connected with the building or the rocket. There had been many people there, a great massed crowd all gathered in the white sandy field, to watch the ceremonies - though, naturally, they were removed before the rocket was launched. I knew that my part in this had been meant to help reconcile the public to this event. It was showmanship for the purposes of state ritual. The real work of activating the crystals was done by those far above me in the priestly hierarchy. I had no idea how it was done and had not seen the crystals, and could only make guesses as to what went on. I was also not given the real information about why the rocket had been launched. I was just told, like everyone else, that it was an experiment and was meant, if successful, to begin to reconnect us with the places of our ancestors amongst the stars. My resentment was general. I loathed the priesthood, of which I was a part, and all of its aims. I judged it to be hypocritical. Fine words were said about healing (and healing work was being done, on a small scale). Behind that, our temple was aligned with a corrupt state. We blessed and condoned what we were told to by the temporal authorities. We - or the higher and more skilled priests - turned out magical and psychic knowledge to debased ends, militaristic and exploitative. The Atlantean Empire was enormous, and those who were in control wielded power on a vast scale. It was somehow this which seemed to be the insanity at the core of Atlantis, not just a longing for wealth and an easy life, for life had been easy and pleasant for a long time. But a crazed desire for extreme power and a deadness to the feelings of others, a dehumanizing of other people.

Individuals and their families were not consulted. If the priesthood had marked you for purposes of their own, you were not asked what you thought. Your life force could be taken (not always so crudely as by the spilling of blood) for the purposes of magico-technological work and you yourself left afterwards as a burned out shell, much the same as that building, and yet still alive. There was censorship of speech and punishment of 'heresy'. (People just 'disappeared'.) It was all justified by the apparent ease and wealth with which we lived - and the glory of the Empire - and the duty we were told we owed to the deities. However, I had come from another part of the land, where values were different, and I judged by the standards I was brought up with, and by my own idealism. Beside that, censorship or not, there were whispered criticisms. Rumours abounded of priests and priestesses who opposed the corruption, though most said that these, horrified at the misuse of their sacred knowledge, were now leaving. They could find no redress in Atlantis and prophesied widespread disaster.

You could trust nobody. Your informant who spoke of rebellion could well be orthodox and turn you in. And all the while we were told of our great good fortune in being of so magnificent a people - the greatest and most powerful the Earth had ever known. Those who talked of abuse and criticized the state policy were denigrated as neurotic prophets of doom or as evil scare-mongers undermining morale. (We were always being told that we had to be on our guard against evil - which was perceived as a sort of soft, glutinous psychic force - enervating and effeminate.)

These memories were very hard to uncover. I felt a reluctance to recall this particular life.

The temple led off the blue corridor - but a long way from the rocket site. It was a very high building with tall windows that seemed to be glazed, like our own present-day ones, but were made from clear crystal. We priestesses had to stand before them and 'receive' the Sun. There were long cushions on recessed benches along the walls. People lay on them to enter a trance state or to be given healing. There were lots of priestesses. Like the others, I wore (strangely) a grey robe and turquoise blue cloak for most everyday work. (I say 'strangely' because in magical colour symbolism, red, orange and yellow are linked with the Sun, for obvious reasons.) I was about twenty years old.

Normally, my work was to assist at ceremonies and also to absorb solar energy into my body and then disperse it in healing and consecration. I hated this work, except for the healing of small children. The priestesses were treated like objects. We were not all suited to that much solar power and some of us suffered exhaustion and illness, because we were asked to conduct more energy than our systems would stand. (These 'burn outs' were followed by rest and recuperation, but they were not good for us.) I, myself, knew that I would have been more suited to work in a Moon temple, notwithstanding that the Sun could be worshipped as a female deity and that many women had a strong solar aspect within their own nature. I was very clearly a lunar type. However, you were not given a choice. You went where you were sent! So I did the work and suffered from it, and yet was passably competent, much to my surprise.

There was no one in the temple who meant much to me, personally. I kept myself aloof. And I had no lover among men or women, not even in my work. There seemed to be no equivalent of the Hieros Gamos, no Great Rite with a priest. Or, if there was, I do not remember it.

There was a man that I loved. But he was many miles away in the Temple of the Stars. We never saw each other at all. He came from the same far away region where I was born and we had been together in childhood and adolescence. But when we were ordained, we were sent to separate places. There was no appeal against this. You just went where the priesthood had decreed, based on their supposed judgement of your abilities.

Many years passed, during which I was silently rebellious but could find no way out. My family was far away and I hardly ever saw them. There was no one to turn to. Then, in my late thirties, I was given different duties and sent from the temple. I had been, in a way, promoted - or perhaps pensioned off! I was now in a much cooler climate, a lot nearer my old home. The building where I stayed was a retreat house of a sort of triangular or wedge shape. There were wooden panels inside on the ground floor, large ones with carved trees on them, and the branches came right out into the room. There was also a big fireplace, comfortable furniture and a highly polished floor. Atlantis, in its last years, was both smart and luxurious. The entire top floor seemed to be for dove-cotes, or to house birds of some kind.

This place was far less formal than a temple, and dedicated to the deities of Earth. Priests and priestesses came to it from every kind of centre. It was used for retreat and also for private 'conferences' - off the record meetings and discussions of one kind or another. It was very out of the way and remote from any city. To my delight, the man I loved from the Temple of the Stars had also been sent there.

He was often in a small room like a kind of conservatory, apparently preparing something out of herbs and oils. But it was more than herbalism, it was some kind of 'alchemy'. It was not what he was meant to do. This was irregular. Straightforward herbalism for healing would have been acceptable, but not this. He'd hidden it under the appearance of something else, some kind of priestly hobby. Few people knew of it and, luckily, we were a long way from the big temples. He and I had long talks about the system we worked in and encouraged each other's rebellion and affirmed each other's ideas. There were also a few others in the retreat house who felt as we did and whom we could trust.

Later still in that life, we had left and were travelling on horseback. We were no longer in priestly costume but wore thick brown winter cloaks over the simple unbleached and rough woven clothes worn by farming people in that region. I had mittens, too. We were both very happy. There were a few other people with us and we had all left the religious organization we had been part of.

After a year or two of the travelling life, relying upon the hospitality in the villages we came to, my lover and I parted from the others who had been in our group. We had plans to approach the higher echelons of the religious order we'd worked for, to try to influence them, and through them, the state. He believed that the corruption could be changed, if they were shown new ways of doing things. He had with him, inside his tunic in a bottle, a clear liquid. It had healing powers, but more than that it indicated a transformative energy of which he had the secret. This was the substance he'd been working on. Only he really knew all about it and its implications. But I understood that the use of it (and of the processes which produced it) would mean it was no longer necessary to overstrain the priesthood, for so-called healing purposes. Much more than that, it actually represented a whole new way of relating to nature, without ruthlessness and without exploitation. Now we wouldn't have to hurt people or the land, to gain the energy with which to fuel state projects. He believed passionately that people only needed to be shown another way and there would be change. He was very unworldly.

The others in our group didn't want to try this. They just wanted to leave, so we parted company.

The priest of the Stars and I entered a small valley where there was a wooden building low down on a slope. (There were other buildings behind it but I couldn't see them clearly.) At the bottom of the valley there was a circular paved area, and behind it another rectangular one, also paved, in which there was a large metal statue of a bird with out-stretched wings.

In front of the wooden house stood a monkish-looking man, robed in grey, with a hood. He was holding an axe. Other men, dressed in the same way, were watching us from the hilltop. I could see that the man with the axe had recognized us. He was someone who had liaised between the retreat house and the temples. And then I knew we had no chance. They would want to make scapegoats of us, a renegade priest and priestess. It might have gone easier if we were of the laity, but we were not. My lover walked up to him, taking the bottle from his tunic. He had carried it safely through our travels and he knew all its secrets.

After that, I saw nothing but blackness. I knew what had happened next but didn't want to relive it. In my twentieth century body, I began to sob. 'I can't leave him. I won't. Look what they are going to do to him.'

My partner, who was helping me with this trance recall, suggested that I come back to the present day. 'Come back. Leave it there.'

I knew that they had executed my lover in a particularly terrible way. They had disembowelled him and made me watch. Later, I also was killed, but less publicly. They didn't care about his 'alchemy'. They simply wanted to stamp out rebellion. And they used our spilt blood for corrupt magical purposes - his disembowelling, and mine, to empower their plans. I couldn't bear to remember it graphically, visually. But I remembered the facts.

After this, I felt violently sick. And the next day, on waking, I still felt very sick and tearful and depressed. The sickness continued for about eight days, on and off. I kept remembering his innocence. And I knew I had been pregnant with his child at the time they disembowelled me.

During that eight days, I did some scrying in black glass, looking for images to explain my state. Instead, these words came. 'There is a woman who is widowed. She is hooded and cloaked in black in her soul. She was widowed for only a few days before she, too, died. But her grief extends across many thousands of years. And the grief distorts her. That woman is myself.'

On some deep level, I had blamed myself for what had happened to my lover, for not advising very strongly against any attempt to win round the authorities. For having initiated our escape. We might have stayed in the retreat house, in a much stronger position. I knew that he hated the corruption as much as I did. But he hated the routine of the priestly life much less. Of course, this guilt was an inappropriate response. I know that now - but it took the recovered memory to show me. At the time, the trauma of what happened twisted my feelings. I had to suffer the worst fate that can happen to anyone, anywhere: to be made to watch while the person who means most to you is brutally put to death. My own death, not very long after, was nothing by comparison. I did not want to live.

I do not know how long it was after this that the end came for Atlantis. Other psychics have said that the corruption was appalling. Some have mentioned experiments in genetic engineering. I have not remembered this myself. But in view of what I did see, I can well believe it. The misuse of magic disturbed the Earth's energies, so they say, and Atlantis was overwhelmed by fire and flood. The whole continent now lies on the sea bed. It seems to me that the Queen of the Dead took Atlantis to Herself, to heal and make new that which had been spoiled, the essence of a once balanced spiritual Way, in a once sacred place. For the balance between male and female had been lost. The Feminine Principle was no longer being honoured equally with the Masculine - and the true Masculine had been discounted in favour of patriarchal thought forms, worshipped as gods. This is true and a fact, for I know, I was there. The results in terms of human misery and exploitation of nature were already obvious. And Atlantis, according to legend, never did find harmony again. There was no feminine nurturing or care for people for their own sake, their personal feelings and needs, but an obsession with power and use of any living creature or the purpose of moral expediency. This was called being rational. It was considered an unsentimental approach that brought (supposedly) the best life for the majority.

That which I have just recounted was so unpleasant to me that I found great difficulty in returning to it. Our attempt to change things in Atlantis was valiant, though naive, and not thoroughly wasted, for we kept some kind of flame alive by the mere fact of our trying. Sometimes, this has to be enough. But I do not recall that life in any real detail. For instance, I do not know what the deities' names were, nor do I have any idea where this Sun temple was. It bears no relation to what Plato described as the main temple of the capital city on the island continent, for though gold and other precious metals were used lavishly in the making of cups, knives and other ritual tools, and the windows of the building were of crystal, I do not remember extreme opulence. (There *was* a kind of pretentiousness - our robes for special occasions were incredibly ornate - and there was a lack, in the style of building, of grace or humility.) It may have been some way from the capital or in another region. Whatever or however we can begin to remember, the story of Atlantis has great value for us today. Many lands have been submerged through natural catastrophe. Atlantis is a prime example (one of the best known) of a great civilization that is said to have destroyed itself.

As to the personal effect on those who once lived there, well, I have met other former Atlanteans who carry in their souls a great wound of disillusionment. Such people are often very gentle, but give the impression that the world is too much for them. And those who once misused Atlantean magic? Their present-day path seems much too obvious to need mentioning.

So what would have been the right response of the people of Atlantis, if they had all known of the danger to their continent, in the way that we now know of the danger to the Earth? This is a big question, only really answerable by a silent pause . . . We have the option of making our views known politically, which they did not. What they could have done was to pray to the Dark Goddess to purify their land and their lives of all that threatened life by disturbing nature's balance. And perhaps they could have worked magic, as we can now for the Earth, in our own age. Even a totalitarian regime is vulnerable to miracles! It all depends on whether the collective desire for justice and freedom and for the health of future generations is strong enough to outweigh evil, and to pray and work magic sincerely for change.

A Spell to Purify the Land of What Harms It

Place before you a lit candle, some paper, a pen that writes in red ink, a dish made out of some non-flammable material (like glass, metal or pottery) and a crow's feather.

Call upon the Dark Goddess to be with you, using your own words, in silence or out loud. Then ask Her to work the magic of transforming all within the land that is harmful to nature. Pause for a few moments as you feel Her draw near to you. Now list on the paper the main things you can think of that hurt the environment. You can mention qualities like greed and exploitation and also physical facts like acid rain, too many cars on the roads, cutting down of woodland, and so on.

Take the crow's feather and circle the paper with it, nine times, counter-clockwise. Say,

'May the land be purified of these ills. By the power of the

Dark Goddess, may human practices and techniques that harm the balance of nature become new ways of harmony and wisdom.'

Next, speak aloud some specific examples (or say them to yourself).

'Polluting methods of transport to be replaced by clean ones.
Greed to become contentment in sharing.
Chemical fertilizers to become organic.'

You can go through all the items on your list in this way.

Hold the paper in both hands, silently dedicating it to the purpose of the spell and imbuing it with your desire for the land's health. Then burn it in the candle flame. As it burns completely away, say 'So May It Be.' (This is a traditional Wiccan ending to any spell.) Collect the charred bits in the bowl that you have ready, and later bury them.

Afterwards, dedicate yourself to purging your own life of at least one of the items on your list and thus transforming it, replacing the old harmful way with something environmentally harmless, or gentler, or more energy-efficient. For example, you might give up your car and use public transport. Or, if this is not possible, stop using chemical sprays in the garden and use organic products instead. Or insulate your home so that you need to use less fuel for winter warmth, or wear more layers of clothing, for the same reason. Your chosen action reinforces your spell and in itself becomes magical, because it is an offering. You may already be doing a great deal in this way, for many people have now begun to make the point to governmental and commercial authorities by changing their own lives. But see if you can find one more thing, because the difference this time is that it is done on a magical basis. It is an empowered act, magically, as well as politically.

Magic works because it is (a) an assertion of your own will for change, (b) an invocation of psychic influences and (c) a ritualized prayer. None of this will convince a confirmed sceptic. I can only say, try it with something more immediate. You will get a result unless there is some good reason why you should not, like an unconscious desire within yourself not to have to make the relevant changes, or else a counterforce from someone else's will. The only question to ask before casting a spell, apart from 'Am I sure this will cause no harm to another being?', is 'How much do I want this?'

But magic does not make any of us all-powerful. It cannot create an individual who asserts her or his will over all other factors and creatures. That is because it fits in with the tides and trends of life. It is neither more nor less effective than other kinds of action. (Its advantage is that when other modes of expression have been removed, this one is usually still there!)

Paradoxically, people report that they never feel so much in communion with the unseen forces of life, never feel less alone, than when working magic for healing purposes. (Perhaps that is the difference between what they used to call 'white' and 'black' magic. The one unites us with all beings and the other separates us from them.)

All life is made up of small deeds that together can constitute a great change. All oceans are small drops in one place. We should never underestimate the power and influence of our small spells, however, inadequate they might seem to be.

My companion and lover in the last days of Atlantis is known to me now. His reaction to the trauma we shared then has been different to mine. Partly, this is due to an innate difference in temperament, and partly to the influences in our subsequent lives. My response, though delayed, was to be drawn towards people similar to the nomads of my first (recalled) Atlantean life: tribal people, more earthy and less power enthralled. Or more honest, as I saw it, and too enamoured of living sensually in the present moment to deploy any long-term strategies for dominance or anything really wicked on a grand scale. I saw and still see this as preferable to the attitudes of people who can ruin a whole land (a whole planet!) by their attempted control of nature, in themselves and in general. When a refined, subtle, self-controlled type goes bad, it can be a medium for evil of frightening dimensions.

My lover, on the other hand, grew more unworldly than ever, in a different style than my own. His psychological reaction was to dislike and fear all life on Earth. He remembers an ancestral and former-life origin on another world than this. A birthplace 'in the stars'. A home planet where gentleness had been more in evidence, at least when he lived there. And he measured corruption on Earth against this memory and tried to hold himself withdrawn from all that he saw as being 'base impulses'. (This is as I understand him. He might tell it differently.) He aimed to become more refined as a spirit, to reach skyward and transcend evil. Symbolically, he wanted to return to the Source, and to goodness. I aimed to return to the roots of Earth life and learn simplicity. We each had a point. If we all could live rooted in the Earth and yet transcend evil . . . His essential nature before the execution was fervently hopeful and idealistic, but his faith and innocence were terribly abused.

As I said, he is someone whom I have met in this life. I will call him J. When we first encountered each other, the repercussions were huge. Though very unlike one another, in present-day background and beliefs, the attraction and deep understanding were immediate, as was the recognition. But, as time went by, we also discovered in each other traits and values that were not just different from our own, but innately hostile. Puzzlingly, the relationship remained compulsive and the joy in one another's existence was as genuine. This put an incredible strain on my marriage, as meetings with former-life lovers and partners so often can. And it seemed to be a final straw in his own relationship with his (then) partner. But the link has continued through all kinds of difficulty and conflict, as well as disturbing revelations about present-life circumstances. It is a non-sexual relationship (or, anyway, non-consumated) yet more disturbing than any love affair I've known. We each sensed the other's existence before we had met and I have no doubt we'd continue to be soul-connected if we said goodbye. Out of this has come, for me anyway, recovery of a past life memory which explains a lot. For one thing, I have, in this life, a disability connected with that experience. As already mentioned, I have not been able to give birth naturally, due to a narrow pelvis, and have twice had to have a caesarean section. And in only one other life that I can remember, have I borne any child. And then only one. Otherwise, so far as I know, I have been childless or had stillbirths. I needed to remember the wound, and the terrible guilt and the deep mistrust of life, which caused my spirit to be born over and over again, with an inhibition and corresponding physical difficulty in becoming a mother.

All our present-day circumstances and physical state, at birth, result from our former existences, individually and collectively.

When I met J. the pain in my womb (severe at each menstruation) became dreadfully increased - for the memory was stirred, unconsciously at first. I had initially had this problem following the birth of my second child, and was then healed by a friend who practised homeopathy. Some years later the pain came back, with excruciating force. And this began to happen around the time of a strong psychic meeting with J. (Before we had met physically, he had the traumatic experience of a car crash, and I felt it happen to him.)

I had previously been uneasy with the very name of Atlantis, already associating it with evil, because of the famed wrong-doing of its last days. Under the stimulus of meeting J., I found out the more personal reasons for my aversion. Then finally, this winter, I responded to inner guidance to look further back in that continent's history, to an earlier life there. I found a spiritual homeland - and fresh self-understanding and inspiration. Since then, I have known an increasing benefit from both homeopathic remedies and herbal treatment. The pain level is decreasing, in spite of the fact that I have suspected endometriosis. And I am quite sure that whatever the organic explanation for my problem, the true inner causes behind the physical disorder, lie in the trauma of having once been disembowelled. They also lie in the guilt and grief I carried, unhealed because previously unremembered, in taking back my spiritual authority as a priestess, as well as in giving birth. This theme for me is so large that I think it could take much of this life to really explore and heal it. But a start has been made.

I am relating this story to share what I have personally learned so far about past-life experiences and present-day conditions.

Not all wounds or illnesses were begun many lives ago. Sometimes, you just break a leg because you do, because today you were careless and stepped off a pavement at just the wrong moment - though arguably that carelessness is caused by some past stress, linking back to very long ago in an unbroken chain ! But when the true causes or seeds do lie in the far past, and physical signs were there at birth, if we had but known it, it does help to understand. In the same way, the reasons for present day aims and skills can be recalled with benefit.

As for the deeper implications for J. of his meeting with me, I cannot write of them. He has not wanted to tell me everything he feels and, anyway, it is his story, not mine to tell.

6

Going To and From the Sacred Island

There are several methods of remembering past lives. One is with the help of a skilled hypnotherapist, using hypnotic regression. This produces a deep trance in which recall is likely to be both dramatic and detailed. However, the completeness with which past experiences can be relived in this way requires the assistance of a *trained* therapist to assimilate and integrate the material, so it is not wise to experiment with it, on an amateur basis, with friends.

On an easier level, there's the Christos method developed by G. Glaskin and described in his book *Windows of the Mind*. This can be attempted by any reasonably well-balanced person, with the help of other people, and has a high success rate, so it is worth considering. A modified version of this is what I have sometimes used.

Thirdly, there are the less complex methods, of which there are several versions, all using similar symbology. There are really very much the same as entry into other kinds of trance or pathworking, but the intention is specific, and so is the request to an inner guide. I find that this sort of thing works very well, and recommend the following.

First, sit in a relaxed position, upright in a chair, your arms and legs uncrossed. Close your eyes and take a few deep breaths and begin to let go of the tensions inside you. Tell yourself that as you count backwards from ten to zero you will relax more and more until you are at peace.

It helps a great deal if you have a friend with you to 'count you down' and to watch over you and direct you in trance. In fact, I do not really recommend that you do this alone, unless you are experienced in inner work and pathworking or meditation techniques. This is in case you remember disturbing events from a past life and feel overwhelmed by them. A friend, at this point, can gently remind you that you are not in that body anymore, and can calmly talk you back through the pathworking routine that restores you (not too abruptly) to your usual state of mind.

Picture yourself surrounded by blue light edged with gold, a great glowing sphere, like the Earth's atmosphere, all around your body and above and below you. Then say a prayer to the Dark Goddess. It could be like this : 'Dark Universal Mother, whose wisdom protects life, I ask you to protect me now from illusion and confusion. Bless my attempt to remember what I need to know of my former lives. And may your love surround me and your truth be in my spirit.'

Pause for a moment and then add, 'I ask now to be within the Inner Realms, in a peaceful sanctuary, where my soul is happy.'

You will find that the blue haze around you then clears and that you are in a scene that brings peace and happiness. This might, for example, be a sun-filled woodland or a temple of some kind, or a cave by the sea. While standing within it, in your imagination, speak silently to your inner guide. (It doesn't matter if you can't see her, or him, they will still hear you, anyway.) Ask to be shown a past life of your own, the one that you now most need to see, for increased self-understanding or renewed health. Then look around you until you see a doorway. If you are in a building it will be, naturally, set into a wall. Outside, the same door may be set into the side of a hill or into a tree trunk. Wherever it is, open it. You will find some spiral stairs going downward.

If a friend is leading you in trance, she or he should suggest all these steps to you. 'Ask to be in a peaceful sanctuary . . . Make a request to your inner guide . . . You see a doorway . . . And a flight of stairs going down . . . etc.' You can also record the instructions on tape and play them back to yourself.

Failures to see anything at all, or the seeing of scenes that do not feel right nor seem likely to lead to the genuine memory of a past life, are usually due to anxiety and tension. Or it may be that you are going through the different stages of entry too quickly. It is a good idea to stay in the peaceful sanctuary until you feel quite used to the trance state. Look around and enjoy trees, green leaves, birdsong, or whatever is there before you ask an inner guide about seeing a past life.

Assuming you feel ready to proceed, you will find, at the bottom of the stairs, an open archway. Once you have gone through it you will have reached the old time and place of your former existence. It may seem very surprising that it could be that simple to return to a time and place before the start of your present life, but after all, all you have done is to jog your *own* memory. The imaginative techniques you have just used, together with the assistance of an inner guide, were merely to recall something that is as much part of you as your memory of being at school or of being a three-year-old. You are not revisiting an old time and place, but remembering. Each one of your memories of any of your lives is yours by right. It is just that we do not remember the former-life ones so easily, as automatic recall might make a new start in this life that much more difficult, so we have to struggle a little, and can do this once a present-life identity is firmly established.

Look down to see what you have on your feet, and then look at your clothes. Try to remember the date and the name of the country. (What comes to mind most immediately is most likely to be true. Hesitation reveals that you are not remembering with accuracy. Do not worry about this as you will relax more and start to see more clearly as you carry on.) Look around you at the landscape. Who are you? What are you doing now? Can you see other people? Animals? What kind of trees, if any? Are there buildings? Are you in a city or in the country? Do not assume that you will see something from long ago. Many people have had former lives in the twentieth century, dying and then being quickly reborn. The gap between lives is known to vary from thousands of years or less than one year. And it is nowadays a lot less than it was in the past. Many souls seem to want to be here now. (Or very many human bodies have been created that need souls, to put it another way.)

Continue remembering until you reach a point where not much is happening. You can then instruct yourself to move forwards in time, to the next important event. Equally, you can first move backwards, to find out the causes of what you have just seen. But - I repeat - all of this is easier if a friend is there to listen to you describe what you have seen (and sensitively to keep silent when you need that!) and above all, to make suggestions about what you should try to find out and whether to move on. Alone, you can get so caught up in what you are seeing that you can forget to find out things that, later on, you'll want to know.

If all goes smoothly, you can explore the whole course of your past life, right up to your dying day. You may not want to experience the actual memory of the moment of death, so you can stop just short of it. But it is instructive to know the manner of your death and the attitudes that you then held. When you feel you have gained all you need or can cope with for now, return - at the speed of thought - to the opening you came through. Climb back up the steps and go out through the door. Step into your sanctuary. Give thanks to your guide and the Dark Goddess for what you have seen. Ask also to be given understanding about what you learned in that life, and the ways you were influenced by that set of experiences. The answer will probably come to you at once. Then visualize yourself once more surrounded by blue light edged with gold and say a second prayer.

'Dark Goddess of Death and Rebirth, may your wisdom go with me and your love surround me. May I now live fully in the present day.'

Return, very slowly, to your usual consciousness.

This is a brief outline of past life recall. If you already have met inner guides and have some psychic experience, it should be enough to proceed with. If not, or if you wish to delve more deeply into the subject, it is worth reading something comprehensive, like J.H. Brennan's *The Reincarnation Workbook*, to get an overview of the many theories and the problems that may be encountered and the practical methods. As well as books on reincarnation, there are also a great many on other people's encounters with spirit guides as well as on their experiences of far memory. Some of these are severely masculist in approach (even when written by women). In these books all the guides are wise men and the deities are all male, and initiates into psychic skills all belong to 'white brotherhoods'! This certainly shows that cultural and religious bias affects inner perception! There have been many generations to whom wise women just could not get through. People's inner eyes were blind to them. It seems that patriarchal assumptions in the seer draw a patriarchal guide. (It is not true to say that all beings in the Inner Realms, including discarnate humans, are always wise.) However, a spirit guide - or someone else's spirit guide - who is on the same 'wavelength' as yourself can give invaluable assistance. And not all books about this subject are masculist.

As I said, there is no final proof of reincarnation. Some have suggested that though the lives we recall are genuine enough, they may not be our lives but a perception of a psychic imprint left by someone else, somewhere on the atmosphere - a sort of natural 'tape' recording of someone's experience. I think this is unlikely, or there would be many cases of people remembering a 'past life' of someone who still lives, and taking it for their own previous existence. (We are, obviously, creating this psychic imprint while we live.)

One last point, on the subject of past lives. Asking to see what you most need to see, that one among all your past incarnations that contains the themes and causes you need to know about, can let you in for surprises! It once resulted, for me, in the recall of a life as a man (unfortunately, the only life in which I have yet remembered being male) who, though English, brought weapons regularly from France to assist the Scots against his own countrymen. In the end, my boat was boarded just off the English coast and I was shot at once. (Justice was rough and quick in those days.) My body was flung into the English Channel where, presumably, small remains of my bones still lie.

I kept no record of this recall, so I do not have much detail (nor have I ever returned to explore it thoroughly). But I know my assistance of the Scots was politically and religiously motivated as much as it was a commercial enterprise. I was in rebellion against English tyranny. There may also have been more personal reasons for what I did.

Interestingly, I still have a residue of his guilt inside me, my former self asking, as he often did, 'Is it ever justified to turn traitor to your own nation, in however good a cause?' Nowadays, in terms of the One-World consciousness we all need, and even in obvious terms of straightforward morality, I find his question archaic. In fact, what I have is not so much guilt as a memory of a past moral dilemma, one which now seems irrelevant but formed a whole way of life, and death, at that time.

The Nature of the Dark Goddess's Realm

As well as remembering past lives, it is also possible, through prayer and meditation, to visit that realm of death - the Dark Goddess's land, the Dark Moon of existence - that lies between lives. There is really quite a lot of information available about what this place is like. The Egyptian and Tibetan Books of the Dead, ancient Greek writings, Druidic tradition, Hindu scriptures and the esoteric factions of Christianity, Islam and Judaism all contain descriptions of the interlife. Most say that the presences to be seen there seem to consist only of colour and light, like a rainbow with no density. It is also sometimes stated (by the Tibetan Book of the Dead, for example) that the entities within the Otherworld take on the shapes and colours we best understand, in terms of our own religious and psychological imagery, in order to translate their meaning to us. There are certain unalterable qualities and processes within this realm, but the way in which we think we see them is very much conditioned by our own expectations and cultural assumptions. The differences-in-similarity between various religions' accounts make this clear. It is borne out by information supplied by people who have remembered the interlife, under hypnosis.

The realm within death's darkness holds infinite light, in much the same way as the darkness of sleep holds dreams or the world of meditation behind closed eyelids holds brilliant visions.

People who have been able to recall this place, under hypnotic regression, confirm that while you see as you expect to see there is also the crossing of a barrier of some kind, which leads to the universal experience of reviewing the former life. This happens in the presence of guiding spirits or deities who help the person to assess their own spiritual development and to understand the effects on themselves and others, of decisions and actions in the recent life. Again, the *appearance* of these figures coincides with the belief system of the individual. Inner guidance has been given to some psychics, explaining that such beings do not have an appearance, in any fixed sense, and also are outside or beyond any exclusive religious belief system. They are simply universal powers and guiding spirits. However, the imagery of human religious traditions is a medium through which they can make themselves understood, in the terms most comprehensible to the spirit to whom they are appearing. This truth, if divulged to those who would like to believe that there is a One True Way in human understanding, would probably be a great disappointment. But it seems to me to make sense. It would seem to indicate that there could be no final or ultimate religious expression, anymore than there could be one final art form or style in art, solely valid and supreme. All our efforts are of worth. (Such a truth, if accepted worldwide, would be immensely freeing to the human spirit, as well as ending religious wars overnight!)

The reviewing process and self-assessment are reputedly common to all. The same process is described, in varying terms, in most religious traditions of every race.

There can also be a choice of whether to plan the next incarnation, in rough outline, with regard to aims in personal development or service, or to dip into it randomly and see what happens. All hypnotized people report the pre-eminence of choice.

Therefore some people prefer to be passive and seem quite disinterested in their own progress. This is a matter of motivation and temperament.

Another universal report is of the great beauty and peace of the Otherworld, once the initial stages have been passed. Love prevails and is everywhere, an atmosphere of unfailing love. Even those who feel they have done much wrong in a former life speak of being accepted with compassion. There is no hell in existence, no place of punishment, except that created by our own anguish when we have to face what we have really done in our worst moments and fully understand any pain that we have caused. That and the shadows created by our own fears (our own 'demons') are all there is of punishment: our remorse and our self-created nightmares. Retribution and the reaping of what we have sown happen to us in the *living* world, because of the ongoing laws of cause and effect, and also, sometimes, because of our very own desires to 'make it up' to others. There is suffering in plenty while we live, but not when we die. Nor is there any need to know esoteric words of power or magical formulae, in order to placate either gods or demons, and procure a safe passage through the Inner Realms. (Such beliefs seem to be the horrific projections of superstitious and fear-ridden people.) In reality, there are kindly spirits to assist and guide us at every stage, so long as we will accept help. This is what hypnotized persons and many psychics have reported.

The love given and received there is ecstatic communion, like that which we experience in complete sexual ecstasy. Yet this is not sexual. It is, however, like that which we can find within sexuality, and in other ways too, while we are still incarnate. Not just an extreme of sensual pleasure but the deep psychic fulfilment of the blending of subtle energies with one we love. In certain stages of the Otherworld, this experience is continuous, an ongoing bliss, or so it is related by spirit mediums and people under hypnosis and in many of the world's religious teachings. But this lovely healing and inspiring state is not experienced by the earthbound. So my statement that processes undergone by the dead are universal is somewhat misleading. It would be more true to say that such happiness is available to all, if we are able to accept it. The earthbound are the folk who, for various reasons, do not fully accept or understand being dead. Sometimes this may be because death happened very suddenly, as the result of an accident. And sometimes, as is fairly well known, it is because the departing soul does not *wish* to depart. A third category of the earthbound are those for whom the full awakening into death's realm of pure spirit life is, at the present time in their development, beyond their psychic reach. The result appears to be that they simply reincarnate with few plans or clear motivations, in the same geographic location where they died. That is to say, they have preoccupation and desires, but usually no life plan or personal quest for self-development or understanding. Such plans as they do have are always connected with people or projects from the previous life, in a very direct way. These may be concerned with the seeking of justice about a particular event, or with revenge or, more altruistically, with a desire to be a comfort to parents whose child has just died. (Of course, the last-mentioned belong in the category of those not wishing to depart. They are not necessarily in the third category as well.) For a full explanation of incomplete entry into the spirit realm, I recommend Hans TenDam's book *Exploring Reincarnation*. His material is drawn from empirical research rather than abstract theory and is very comprehensive.

Any one of the dead who has entered into the spirit realm completely can be in communion with another spirit, by a means which is like telepathy but is beyond words. The quality of love which sustains and permeates these relationships is that of the deities. It *is* the deities. This is felt to be a love and a Presence beyond either gender and yet containing both. Scriptural views about which, if either, is the supreme power, once Goddess and God can be differentiated, quite naturally vary with place and tradition. (Hypnotized present-day subjects gave no views on this, except to describe themselves also as spirits who contained qualities of both genders, and yet seemed to be beyond both.) However, the interlife as a place is often referred to in feminine terms as a womb, rather as the land is known as our Mother in this life. In Neolithic cultures, the equation was made between tomb and womb by the burial of the dead in a womblike structure, painted with red ochre, to symbolize blood. Neanderthals buried their dead in a foetal position, seemingly in preparation for rebirth.

My own guides tell me that, on one very important level, the Otherworld *is* the Dark Goddess. She is the womb, as the womb is an expression of Her creativity and psychic power of manifesting Her dreams. She is the place itself, as well as being in it. Yet the God is also present in the Otherworld. He stands within the visionary realm as Guardian and as Psychic Begetter, for He makes Her dreams fertile. This is why the Otherworld is beyond gender, for there is between Them such perfect harmony and integration as to make of Them almost one being.

A great magic will be done, of healing and transformation, when once the world of the living has reached the same loving balance between masculine and feminine as is found in the spirit world, yet within bodies that are not physically androgynous but gender specific.

Some of the visions described in scriptures and mythology and folk-lore and confirmed by people under hypnosis are also shared by those who have been briefly pronounced clinically dead, and then resuscitated. There is not, of course, the planning for another life, but glimpses of the Realm of the Dead, startling in similarity from person to person. Common factors include being drawn down a dark tunnel and into a golden light. In my teens, I once painted a picture of this scene. I had never read anything, then, about death's realm or other people's visions, so it must have been from spirit-memory, though I don't know what triggered it. There's a wonderful similarity between this tunnel and the birth canal - as though death were another kind of birth, which indeed it is. As though we are born into the Dark Goddess's womb, Her great Sea of Light, as well as born from it. The difference, unhappily, is that too few babies are born into beauty and tranquillity and warm golden light. It's more often the cold white glare of a hospital room and an atmosphere of excitement but also pain, at least in modern western culture.

It appears that in the Otherworld we all go through certain archetypal experiences, as in dreams. And, exactly as in dreams, or in the world's mythologies, these experiences are portrayed to us in terms of either our own personal or our culturally formed imagery. The situations and their meanings are universal, but most of the symbols through which they are presented to us are not. However, some symbols are more generally perceived than others, and it would seem that these are the ones drawn directly from human experience of our own biology or most basic needs.

What emerges about the interlife, beyond questions of interpretation of different religious traditions, is its joyousness. And we all belong *there* as well as here. The deep, innermost dimension or essence of each one of us is of that place. We are of the Source. So, too, are the nature spirits, animals, plants and stones. The deities shine in and through life in all its forms, which is why contemplation of beauty in a landscape or a tree or a flying bird or a human smile or a piece of music or the line of a poem reawakens our eternal spirit. Perception of the divine quality in others is the connective power which makes our world whole and ourselves at one. (But of course we do not analyse it or name it while it is happening. It is beyond words.) The gift of divinity in others is to enhance, when we recognize it in them, the divinity within ourselves. And from that state of deep, inner connectedness - and love - we can bring healing, in subtle ways. We can mediate the Dark Goddess and help to heal what is sick or distorted or suffering. This is what healers do when they 'channel the spirit', for the Source of this shining life is in the spirit realm. What we see in the beauty of a living landscape or another person has its origin within the Otherworld, in eternity.

None of this has anything to do with patriarchal traditions of pious hymn-singing in heaven or burning in hell. Nor is it remotely connected with concepts of demonic forces striving to ensnare the unwary soul. The Dark Goddess says, without any words, that Her realm, where all paradoxes are resolved and all opposites reconciled, lies far beyond any human misunderstanding. She counsels a feeling approach and true tolerance. Her spiritual domain transcends religious traditions and yet runs like an unspoken sympathy beneath them all.

The essence within ourselves which is of the Otherworld, not transient but of an eternal nature, is not peripheral to manifest reality but the vital centre of it. It is what continues after death and is reborn, expressing itself in form after form. By acknowledging it as 'the centre', we can not only honour its creative function in life but avoid hierarchical or Earth-disdaining concepts about where we go to after we're dead. We can cease to see it as 'above us'. Old-fashioned religious symbolism has long described 'heaven' and 'the spiritual' as height and elevation, a state of being 'above' all natural instincts and, simultaneously, sort of 'up in the sky'. Nowadays, it is more accurately said that the divine is met with by going downwards or deep within. Concepts of either height or depth may be misleading. The spirit, or spirit realm, is at the centre, from which all else emanates in concentric ripples. That centre is so small, yet it is omnipresent. It is unlocatable in physical terms and yet, mysteriously, it is infinitely vast. It is both the Goddess and the God within, and it is also Their country.

The central essence of a being is what lives at the Dark Moon, between the light and the light of different incarnations. It is of the Otherworld, the sacred place of the ancestors where we go to beyond each death, a place we cannot only remember (by certain techniques) but where we can always visit - at least to the borders - in meditation and light trance.

Inner Journey to the Dark Goddess

Close your eyes and relax. Surround yourself by blue light edged with gold and say a prayer for protection. Then ask to be within your sanctuary, where your soul is at peace. Spend a short while there, just simply enjoying it.

Now look around till you see flowing water. (You may hear it first.) If your sanctuary is a building, you will need to go outside for this. Follow downstream until you come to the sea, which will not be too far away. While standing upon the shore, make this invocation:

'I call to the Ferryman of Souls. In the name of the Dark Goddess, may He come to me now, to take me in His glass boat to Her Sacred Island. Without harm to myself, may I visit Her realm and then return safely to my present life.'

You will see a magic glass boat coming across the sea. It is piloted by a dark-cloaked man, who approaches the shore. (Use your magic mirror here, to verify His identity.) Go with Him in the boat and be ferried to an island. When you step ashore, look around for a cave. There will be one in the cliff face, not far from where you land. Go inside and walk into the twilight of a long chamber. There may be bones or other signs of death to either side of your path. Do not be afraid of them. You are protected. They are only symbols of the disintegration that attends upon the body when the spirit has left.

At the back is a short, dark passage. You bravely walk into it and then find that the other end opens out into a place of soft, golden light. Stepping through, you go into a garden of healing herbs. Enjoy the subtle fragrances and sights and sounds. See if there is any one herb that especially attracts you. There may be bees flitting from flower to flower. There will be an atmosphere of great peace.

Say a prayer. Something like this.

'Dark Mother (or here name the Goddess, if you have a name for Her), may I be in your presence. May your love surround me. Awaken my eternal self, in communion with you. Regenerate me, as a being of inner beauty. For just as you are Queen of the Dead, so you are Lady of Rebirth. Remake me in beauty and strength. Restore me to new life. Bless also and heal . . . (here, name all those known to you who need healing). Let them walk a path of happiness.'

After a pause, end with something like this: 'It is well and all will be well, by the Lady's will. For happiness and well-being in all creatures is Her desire.'

Now walk onwards into the garden, to a sea of light. Somehow, the Earth below your feet grows less dense. Very gradually, it becomes transparent and then ceases altogether. You are walking on an ocean of gold light. It upholds you and is also around you. Within this, you may see either a vision of the Goddess or a spirit presence or you may hear a message. If

She blesses you with a complete sense of an inner communion with Her, stay with the experience until it begins to ebb. Whatever you see or hear of good, give thanks for it and then return to the garden.

If by any chance you see anything that disturbs you, be assured that it is not a messenger of the Goddess. Even while venturing, like Psyche, within the Otherworld, we remain as incarnate and subject to confusion. Use the mirror to confront the disturbing entity and, as you see it vanish, pray to the Goddess for its healing. It may be a nightmare projection of what you, or others, have feared and also suppressed within. Or it may be of another order of being - a 'malicious sprite'. Remember, you are not now in the Inner Realm of discarnates, but in a particular psychic emanation *of* that. Therefore, you are not in the Place where all beings are in harmony, but on the side of the living, when it comes to the universal barrier and border. This is a sort of intermediary place where the living and dead can meet. It is also where we can meet with or commune with deities and guiding spirits and with beings of another order, less dense than our own, yet still incarnate. (To actually cross the border and be in the central realm is forbidden to the living. Yet we can get close enough to it to understand it.)

Once in the garden again, you can spend a few moments in thinking about your own life - just how you feel inspired to live, as your own unique self. Call upon the All-Father. You may have already communed with Him while in the sea of light, but if not, then invoke Him now. Say something like this:

'Divine Lord in the Darkness, Bright One of the Otherworld, by whom we each live as a wanderer through time, touch my being with your love, that I may make real, within time's stream, all that I have envisioned of beauty and harmony.'

Pause, while you feel His approach in your own innermost being. You may also see a vision or be told something.

When you are ready, go back down the passageway and out through the cave mouth. The Ferryman (the All-Father in a different guise) will be there waiting for you. Go back across the water. Thank Him as you climb ashore. Follow the stream to your sanctuary. Then, with a final prayer for protection, surround yourself with the blue sphere of light and return to usual consciousness.

Take your time about coming back. You have been a very long way into Inner Realms. What happened to you there will depend on your own inner orientation and can include meetings with the unborn, including those who are future friends or even your own children or grandchildren, or those of people you are close to. This is beyond symbol systems or dogma of any kind (and requires sensitivity and tact if you want to share what you have seen).

In your life, you may now feel, in a new way the touch of the Bright Goddess, the Lady of Creativity and Manifest Beauty. She and the Dark Goddess of Inner Realms are two faces of the same Great Mother. It is vital to understand this, for our journeys to Inner Realms are not meant to be an escape from living but a renewal and strengthening for life.

Transcript of Inner Guidance on the Visit to a Sacred Island

Guide: The Sacred Island is the place in ourselves that is beyond the veil separating the reality of the spirit world from the manifest world. The spirit world is always present, everywhere, but the veil obscures it. Otherwise, the living would not be able to feel fully incarnate, as separate entities. They would always dwell partly within the Otherworld. So that you do not forget, nor lose all communion with the Goddess and God, and so that the powers of healing may be mediated, the veil may be parted sometimes, from either side. The Sacred Island is like all those places on the Earth of which it is said 'the veil' there is thin, meaning that psychic experience comes easily. In reality, the whole Earth is sacred, because everywhere is the body of the Mother Goddess, but there are also especial places that are consecrated to communion with the spirit world of the inner senses. Some are small, like Glastonbury, the Isle of Avalon, or like the island of Iona in the Scottish Hebrides. Some are larger, like the country of Ireland - or like Tibet. These mystical islands or lands (which are 'islanded' even if not physically surrounded by water) are portals to a certain state of consciousness. Within it, people can more easily than usual recognize the spirit presences and even the Divine. They are also the places of many phantasms, therefore it is good to approach them with much spiritual preparation. Though no place exists where you cannot be in contact with the spirits, in these places it is more easy.

Rae: Why are some places on Earth portals? What is it that makes them so?

Guide: They are places of a particular resonance. The *sound* made there by the Earth's pulse, in connection with the flow of invisible energy that you study in Earth Mysteries. It is conducted by the ley lines and is stimulating in a special way - through subtle connections with the endocrine system. This awakens the psyche so that contact is made with the Goddess's healing power and so that spirit messages are heard - familiars, discarnates, faery beings, plant spirits, land elementals or angels. A place is also a portal when its beauty or grandeur or starkness or mystery evoke feelings that are not worldly. I cannot tell you all about this. It is not simple. Sacred geography is a life-time's study. You do not need to know more, for the time being. Such places are everywhere and in all lands. There are the greater portals and also the lesser ones. For example, the entire land of Eire is a lesser portal, but within it there are the greater ones.

Rae: Is it essential for everyone to go on pilgrimage to sacred places? What happens when we cannot?

Guide: It is best if you can do so, sometimes. But making the inner journey in your own home can be as effective. For you turn your own vitality to awakening of the psychic faculties. Though more draining initially, you are rewarded. You will feel the flood of the Lady's healing power through your whole being. But the first result of this, or of an outer pilgrimage, may be to put your life into some crisis. To heal you and bring you back to your own true destiny, you may need to be stripped of something. For example, your place of residence may be unhealthy and it may be for the best if you are forced to move house. Or your form of work or relationships may be distorting you. There may need to be change and loss before there can be new life. Remember, the Dark Goddess's sign is the black feather. Her birds are the carrion. In Her Otherworldy Realm, there is light and fair weather. Yet Her season is winter. Her time is the night. That is why many people fear Her.

Rae: How does an inner visit to the Sacred Island - or an outer pilgrimage - bring about healing? I mean how is it extended from a momentary though profound experience, to something which can lastingly affect life and even bring about change we didn't know we needed?

Guide: The soul gains healing and is restored. Physical death restores vitality to the tired spirit. Loss of consciousness in sleep and dreams restores the body and mind (though dreams sometimes restore the soul, also). Inner journeying and communings in pilgrimage - like art, the result of other people's communings - restore the soul. This is the dimension of deep feeling and imagination that *translates* the spirit through into the body and so into life. Communion with the Dark Goddess of the Otherworld will change life by changing your soul. This rarely happens immediately, because changes that manifest usually happen at the normal pace of material life, rather than (as within the

Otherworld) at the speed of thought. The realm of the body will sometimes take a while to catch up with the soul's change.

Healing is not always achieved. The Dark Mother does not force change upon any soul, no matter how beneficial change would have been. That is the law of existence, because you are a separate entity. She restores and generates anyone's soul, in so far as there is no resistance to that healing, no rejection of the necessary changes in life that would result from it. And therefore She increases your inner strength and renews hope. When you pass on the love and wisdom received in the Inner Realms, whether in caring for the birds in the hedgerow or your family or friends or strangers in the world at large, through some form of service or creativity or the conscious mediation of spirit healing, then you are further strengthened in yourself. That is another law.

Rae: What happens for those who have little contact with messengers of the Otherworld or the presence of Spirit, either through their religious traditions or through the arts or nature, or in any other way?

Guide: It has been a great tragedy of this Age which is now almost over. A new Way is being sought by millions, for a new Age, so the tendency is being counter-balanced and will become rare, though it is now very common. It is a serious thing, indeed, when a soul goes under-nourished. It weakens, and then can't mediate the true presence of the person's spirit. Nor can that person relate to the presence of the spirit of anyone or anything. So all seems empty of meaning and cynicism sets in. The person's whole life becomes merely a quest for sensory gratification and material security. They have no sense of the sanctity of life and sentimentality and hypocrisy take the place of true feeling and morality. If the slow death of the soul is not halted, the being becomes more unbalanced until the use and abuse of other creatures reaches a peak - a state of complete indifference to others' sufferings and needs. Since the qualifying distinction of a human soul, fully developed, is empathy and imaginative identification with another's situation - caringness - this is devastation indeed. The isolation becomes entire. There is no love. Such a being needs healing, above all. If they are prepared to receive it, as many are, in the end, for they are in great anguish, there is therapeutic power in both nature and art, as well as in other people's compassion and love. Also, there is help from the Otherworld. The spirit messengers are always trying to make themselves known. It is not so very easy to feel love for those who have sick souls and have acted with extreme cruelty. But a work of redemption can be done if this is achieved. It must be distinguished from sentimentality - or from a glossing over of the suffering of victims. At death, the Dark Goddess will take what is left of a fading soul into Her Otherworld. For such beings, this is hard. Some wander, earthbound, for as long as they can. They fear the meeting with who they really are, inside Her realm. The dreaded confrontation with a spirit reality that has been long denied, and with their own spirit. So it is essential for happiness on Earth that every soul is honoured and given true nourishment.

Rae: What happens when a soul dies, completely?

Guide: While the body is still alive but the soul dead, there is possession by a demon. Often this is an entity, a thought form, of great cruelty, something the person may have created by their own past broodings and attitudes. The body continues to live, but possessed by that. Such a fate is terrible beyond all things. After bodily death, which often follows swiftly, such a spirit, one whose body has known this desecration, is returned to the Great Mother for a long span of Earth time, before reincarnation in any form. It has lost the right to an individual soul, and must redevelop one. As an individual human being, it has ceased to exist. Spirit, however, is eternal and cannot cease to be. Therefore, the spirit will become something other than the human in its next incarnate form. I mean something without consciousness of being mortal or individual. It may become grains of sand in a desert or a colony of ants. (It may *not* become something with an equal though different range of responses to the human, like an elf or an elephant.) But the death of a human soul is not something to dwell on. It is my wish to talk about healing. And complete death of a soul is an infrequent occurrence. Even among evil men, there is usually some feeling left, somewhere.

Rae: It *is* an unpleasant subject, but I had to ask! Now I will get back to what I need to know about the presence of a deity. I have been taught to invoke the God as well as Goddess. What happens when we do not?

Guide: Unless you have a resistance, He comes to you anyway. And if He did not, your dreams would prove sterile. It is best for your own development - and for the honouring of the divine in man - if you deliberately invoke Him. Spiritual powers don't go away if we don't call upon Them, but it is best for the well-being of the Earth and ourselves to honour equally the Feminine and the Masculine.

Rae: And what happens if we only call upon the Father?

Guide: Again, the Mother will come to us anyway, if there is no resistance. Without Her, there are no dreams of harmony nor of beauty. Instead, there are fantasies and sickness and distortions. Peace and justice begin to fade. The people become intolerant and harsh and cruel. What they bring forth in the world is an untruth and ugliness. It is born of the head, not the heart.

7

Spell, Shrine and Continuing Story

I t may be that you find it hard to see any visions at all, or to hear inner voices. Here is a spell taught to me by a herbalist who is also a cunning man, for the purposes of developing clairvoyance and all the inner senses. Psychic ability is reduced - for anyone - if we are tired or anxious, but assuming these problems do not exist, the following piece of magic is bound to produce a result in some way. It is also very beautiful. I call it the Willow Spell.

To prepare for it, you should take seven very thin willow wands. Do this without any damage to a tree, by breaking them cleanly from the tips of the branches. Let them dry in a reasonably warm room, until you need them. Preferably, you should gather them at Full Moon.

On the night of the Dark Moon, prepare a plain, dark-coloured mug or small bowl of eyebright tea. (This rite may be done by a group of people or a couple, as well as by one person, but still only one bowl of tea will be needed.)

By eyebright, I mean the herb *euphrasia officinalis*. You can make tea with this by steeping dried eyebright in boiling water, one teaspoonful to each small cup. Let it stand for about fifteen minutes in a covered container, then strain it into your dark-coloured mug or bowl. If you wished to, you could now drink it, or bathe your eyes with it, for medicinal purposes. Euphrasia is used to treat catarrh and all congestive conditions, but more commonly it is known as a specific for inflamed eyes and applied both internally and as a compress. You would want to use it warm, if drinking it, anyway. But for the magical use that I will now describe, it is all right if it cools down.

Dried eyebright is available from many wholefood shops or can be bought, postally, from a large herbal supplier like Baldwin's of London. Fresh eyebright flowers from June to October and is quite common. Nevertheless, you may want to think twice about using it, unless you have it in your garden, as many other wildflowers were once common and now are not!

In a candle-lit room, cast your circle to work in. How this is done has been described in my book *Hedge Witch* and by many other writers, but briefly (and in simplified version) you should mentally surround a circle about six to nine feet in diameter with a glowing sphere of blue light. If you have marked out the circle with chalk or a ring of stones beforehand, so much the better. Then, at each relevant point of the compass, call upon the Guardian Spirits of East, South, West and North to protect and assist you. Call also upon the Spirits of the Centre. (These Guardians of the Five Directions correspond, respectively, to the elemental essences of Air, Fire, Water, Earth and Ether, in magical tradition.)

Within the circle, have a small altar to the Dark Goddess and the Bright Lord in Darkness. Place upon it some incense or joss sticks, two lit candles, a small bowl of water and a stone or dish of earth. Have also a few shells in honour of the Goddess - or any other thing that suggests Her or Her messengers to you. For the God, place a piece of flint or some wood from an oak tree - or whatever feels right to you.

Stand before the altar, facing it, and raise your arms from the elbow, palms turned outward. Say something like this:

'Hail to the Dark Goddess of the Otherworld' (or here name Her if you wish), 'you who are Queen of all psychic sense, by which our spirits know inner truth. Visions in the dark, behind closed eyelids, are your gift. And by these we see beyond the world's mask. Awaken in me the clear seeing by which I may go safely in Inner Realms, and learn what I must learn, to be at one with my destiny and serve the deities' plan for the happiness of all creatures. Grant me also the wisdom to understand what I see. May your blessing be upon me.'

Lower your arms and pause for a few moments. Then raise them again, your palms still outwards, but with the two middle and ring fingers curled down, and held by the thumbs. Say something like,

'Hail to the Bright God in Darkness, the bringer of passion. By you, we dance, we enjoy our time, we bring our gifts to the world with joy and conviction. May I live from the beautiful visions and dreams I may see, and from clear inner knowing. Protector of the Truth, may your blessing be upon me.'

Now take the bundle of willow wands, which should be tied together with a thread of dark wool or cotton. Raise them high at the altar in offering and then pass them swiftly through the incense smoke and the candle flames, then spatter them with a few drops of water and touch them to the stone or dish of earth. At the centre of the circle, upon the floor, should be your bowl of eyebright tea and some matches or a taper. Set fire to one end of the willow wands, so they flame as a torch. Hold them above the dark bowl and watch their reflection in the liquid.

Say, 'As the willowfire to eyebright,
        shining in the dark like Moonlight,
        so may the flame of the Goddess awaken my Sight.'

Plunge the flaming wands in the potion, dowsing them completely. Then bathe your eyes in the liquid and annoint your forehead.

Afterwards, sit comfortably with your eyes closed beside the bowl. (It helps to have brought a cushion into the circle, in readiness for this.) You may not see a vision at once, but gradually you will find that the darkness clears. Do not worry if you don't understand what the pictures mean. Understanding will come later. When you are ready to finish the Seeing, open your eyes and get up very slowly. Return to the altar and, facing it, say something like this.

'I give thanks for the gift of clear Sight and for what I have been shown. May I use my vision well in the service of life. May the blessing of Goddess and God go with me on this night, and in all time to come.'

Thank the Guardian Spirits of the four directions and Centre for watching over you. Then surround yourself with blue light edged with gold. Extinguish the altar candles but leave the incense to burn out.

When I did this spell a few years ago I was rewarded by a vision of the Dark Goddess. As She appeared to me then, She was tall and pale-skinned with long black hair and clear grey eyes. She wore a black cloak over a white robe and black over-dress. Her face was beautiful and fine-boned and Her expression both stern and gentle. She was neither a very young woman nor an old one. On the middle finger, She wore a ring with a transparent stone in it, a quartz crystal, I believe. She stood in a woodland clearing by starlight. At Her feet was a cauldron.

This vision came to me after I heard a voice say, 'First the darkness, then pictures begin to form.'

What I saw had a special clarity. Each detail was distinct, every leaf on the trees, each line of the Lady - Her cloak and long hair. There was a kind of clear, silver-grey light everywhere. I was not 'visualizing' and had made no attempt to picture Her to myself. Instead, Her image appeared with the spontaneity of a dream, yet with much sharper delineation. It was as though what I saw was more real than anything I normally see, either in dreams or in waking life.

Later, in other visions, I saw Her again. She kept coming to me unexpectedly. Always, Her face and manner were compelling. I noticed She wore a brooch, two entwined snakes in silver. Since then, I have seen Her in many guises. Her appearance changes.

Visions may appear, for any one of us, of the Dark Goddess of various traditions, or of the differing guises of the Goddess of one tradition. I would not like to give the impression that She looks just as I saw Her, always. An African Dark Goddess might be a black mermaid, as Yemaya is said to be. Or She could be a black-skinned woman in a blue robe, like the Afro-Brazilian Iamanja. The colours of Her robes may be black, red and white, like those of Kali, but as Tiamat She may be dressed in a cloak of silver scales, a garment of fish skin. It is also quite common for a spirit or deity to appear in vision as a vast figure of shining light, of no discernible colour and of indistinct shape. And indeed, I have seen Her this way, too. There are no fixed rules for a shape-shifting Goddess! You may even see an animal or bird and this may be the Dark Goddess or Her spirit messenger. Or you may not see Her at all, but see something else, like a vision of the past or future of the world, or of something much more personal, your own destiny. Or you may not see much at the time, but later that night, have a guiding dream.

Whatever happens, keep a record of it. Learning to pay attention to dreams, visions and inner voices is always helped by writing about them. A description will focus your attention on what you have seen and heard and help you to remember the details you may not have noticed at the time. If you have not understood the meaning of a vision or message, then you should pray for understanding to the Dark Goddess, in Her aspect of wisdom. The answer may come later on, quite unexpectedly. You may feel a deep certainty, a sudden complete knowing, just as you are, for example, stepping onto a bus!

The best advice I can give for development of psychic skills is to remember and *value* your own intuitions and all inner visions. Most people are far more psychic than they know, but we are taught, as children, to disbelieve our inner knowledge and to regard psychic experience as trivial. By the time that we question this, the harm has been done. We have learned to suppress budding psychic knowledge before it can develop.

Keeping a record of visions and prophecies helps to build confidence. You can look back on past successes, including those visions which you did not understand at the time, but which came startlingly true in the end. These are often messages about some future event, portrayed in symbolic terms. There may also be words, or a sense of just simply knowing what the pictures mean. Our confidence is undermined when our culture tells us that psychic perceptions are a superstitious fantasy and best denied. To look back and find that over and again you were *right* is a good antidote for this. Confidence begins to grow.

A Shrine to the Dark Goddess

You may want to make a shrine to the Dark Goddess in your own home. This can become a focus for your devotions. You can place offerings upon it, such as incense or any art or craftwork. You can stand or sit before it, to pray or meditate. However, you may not wish this to be on full view to all visitors, provoking questions about your beliefs at inopportune moments, or being used as a place to put teacups, gloves or cigarettes. There may be a spare room, or a corner of a bedroom, where a shrine can be placed discreetly. Otherwise, you might think of building, buying or adapting a cupboard or curtained shelf, so that a shrine in your bed-sitting or living room can be concealed.

You will need to place on it objects that symbolize the Dark Goddess and that awaken your inner self in connection with Her. If working in a spare room, or anywhere with sufficient space, cover a small table with a dark-toned cloth. Black or brown velvet look very good. On the left side, arrange a few small bare twigs, to represent winter trees, a number of black crows' or ravens' feathers and some small animal bones, if you can find any while out on a country walk. A hare's skull is ideal, but you may use anything. On the right side, have a living pot plant or fresh flowers, an egg shell and a small piece of fur. The egg shell, for preference, should be a whole one, with the yolk and white blown through. It would not, of course, be appropriate to rob a wild bird's nest for this purpose, so it is perfectly all right to use a hen's egg. But you might be lucky enough to find a large, undamaged piece of wild bird's egg somewhere in a wood, or even your back garden. Another approach is to buy an egg shape made of wood or a semi-precious stone. (I have one made of polished limestone.)

In the centre, place a glass, metal, wooden or pottery chalice, to represent the Grail. This conveys many meanings - the Cup as death potion or healing brew, loving cup or womb or woman's breast. These meanings run the gamut from death to rebirth and are not mutually exclusive, but together convey the Mysteries and power of the spirit realm, seen in the flesh. For different rites, you can focus on different aspects. One day, for example, relating to the Cup as that which brings an ending in some area of your life, and then a new start, another day sharing a drink from it with a lover, in a mutually agreed upon love spell.

On either side of the chalice, place a plain white candle in a simple candlestick. These should be lit every day.

The shrine can now be used for daily prayers, as well as the drinking of blessed water or wine, or for any other healing rites. The left hand side represents death and so purification and the spirit world, and the right represents rebirth. The Cup resolves and unites them, in a whole continuum of sacred meaning, of this world and the Otherworld.

The above is an example of a Dark Goddess shrine, but you may make it as simple or as complex as you like. For example, if you have limited space, use only one twig, feather and bone, instead of several.

If you want to keep a focus on one tradition, like the esoteric Christian, you could have a statue of the Black Madonna placed centrally on a plain wooden table. Put a white candle on each side and a pot or jar of essential oil to the left (preferably myrrh) with a red rose to the right. This flower could be painted or embroidered or carved or made from fabric.

I do not know if small Black Madonna statues can be bought. But if not, you could commission a craftsperson to make one, if you have the money. Or you may have the skills to make one for yourself, or to paint a picture of Her. In the last resort, a framed postcard of a statue would do, flanked by the two white candles.

The same principle applies to a shrine to Isis, Black Tara or any named Goddess, though the objects to right and left would be in keeping with particular traditions.

A very effective shrine can be made to the Mermaid Goddess, as Sea Mother of the World and the Spirit Realm. Drape a table or shelf with a cloth of midnight blue. Place centrally a small black cast iron cauldron, with a white candle to each side. To the left, have a large piece of clear quartz crystal, to the right, a mother of pearl comb. The quartz connects you, through clear-seeing, with the spirit realm of the ancestors, and the comb with the sensual power of the living. (This is a deluxe version and is very expensive. You could make it less splendid but cheaper, with just a dark-coloured cooking pot and a hand mirror to the left and a wooden comb to the right. This will be just as powerful.)

There are no rules for making a shrine, except that it should look and feel right to you. To have one in your home is like inviting the tangible presence of the Goddess into your everyday life. Or, to put that another way, since She is never absent, it is both an affirmation of this and a personal resource, since it makes inner communion with Her much easier. You can place on it incense, water and any requirements for special occasions. You might also want to place something in honour of the God. Flint, to indicate sparks, acorns for His association with the oak or a small model ship to show Him as the Mariner or Ferryman. Whatever seems right to you. A group or family can use the same shrine and it can be unifying to design it together. It is also possible to have one group shrine to the Dark Goddess by a name everyone can relate to - and another to a lesser known or different Goddess, for your personal use. All the Goddesses are one Being, so the shrines are to the same deity, in fact. But people feel drawn to the imagery of one tradition rather than another, for a variety of cultural, emotional and past life reasons. Having more than one shrine acknowledges this and allows both group worship and individual development. It also allows people to visit each other's shrines, within the same home, and so experience different atmospheres of various racial or cultural manifestations of the Goddess or God. Such focal places of worship need not take much space, so your home does not need to be very large to achieve this. It just takes ingenuity.

After Atlantis

To return to the thread of my own spiritual autobiography, I will now explain my response to the death of my old illusions about Atlantean spirituality. What followed the last Atlantean life, at least in my memory, was an incarnation as a priestess from the Middle East, who came to Britain with the priesthood of an invading power. I then met with a young native shaman (my partner in this present life) who taught me tribal magic and his people's beliefs about nature and our place in it. The non-manipulative, non-dominant style of their practices won me round completely, in spite of my nervousness at a primitive and earthy way of life. (More primitive, by a long way, than the Middle Eastern temple culture I had known and grown up with, based, as it was, on the remnants of dispersed Atlantean knowledge.) My disillusion with 'high magic' and sophistication was very deep. I had seen the terrible misuse, not only in a past life, but right then and there in what is now called the British Isles, as the incoming priesthood used the sacred places to empower their selfish schemes and to direct future life in Britain as they saw fit. (This meant hierarchical social and religious structures, unequal division of resources and an insidious and growing exploitation of the land, not only in terms of its physical possibilities, but also for the power-base its strong magnetic-etheric Earth energies could provide. They used magic to direct the subtle currents of the ley lines into powering institutions like militarism. Of course, Britain was not the only land in which this was done, but there was a feeling at the time that these islands were a key place, in terms of world history, for good or ill.)

Their attempted control of the course of fate, though not all-powerful, was intended to exert an influence indefinitely - or at least, for many thousands of years, right up to the present day. The great difference between their attitude and that of the earlier priesthood of the tradition, or of the tribes in Britain at the time, was that whereas earlier people had erected monoliths, cairns or stone circles to enhance and affirm our connectedness with nature and the extra-terrestrial powers (like Sun, Moon and Stars), these people wished only to use the same structures to manipulate or control. Their aims and beliefs were the same as those which endanger all Earth life at this very moment. Crystal magic was used and, at first, I took part in it, to my later shame. I am not saying that the magical use of crystals is evil in itself. But I have seen at first hand how it can be abused. In my life then at Avebury, and later in the area that is now the Chilterns, I had plenty of time to think about this.

It was, as far as I know, my first life in these islands, but it formed in me a very deep bond with them. This place became my new home. It was also my last remembered life as a Pagan priestess. There may have been others, but I have not recalled them. Afterwards, as far as I know, were many lives in Great Britain and Ireland, in which I was involved in the new religion of Christianity. (Of course, this turned up a few thousand years after my life in Avebury, but I have recalled nothing from the interim.) More than once, I was a nun. Also, I was the afore-mentioned Catholic sailor and then an aristocratic lady, staunch Church of England, and then, quite recently, a village school mistress. There may have been spiritual reasons why I needed to go with the current of Christianity for a long while. In turning from the priesthood of which I had been a part, an ethos recognizable in its style and basic assumptions even when corrupt, I had somehow sacrificed my position of power to retain my integrity. I think that was a part of it.

It is also likely that I was motivated by fear. The Inquisition was about to appear on the European scene, so if I had intended to escape to comparative innocence, in a tribal culture, for as long as possible, that option was no longer a safe one. I knew these men already, the witch-hunters. They were the same kind of spirits, if not actually the same beings, as those in Atlantis who dealt with heretics in similar ways. From now on, no priestess nor any village wisewoman would be safe from per-secution. The worship of a Goddess would be outlawed. (In other parts of the world, like India for example, where a priest-ess could still live and work, I had, as far as I know, no bonds or desire or deep feeling or what is called 'karma'. In Britain, on the other hand, I had formed links of love. I had also once done crystal magic on that land mass, to affect the future of that population. And now I felt bound to live with the results of what I had helped to bring into being. My ignorance at the time was an ameliorating factor, but I had still done it. And now I felt involved. So Britain was where I reincarnated, time after time.)

Those who knowingly came to Neolithic Britain as part of a corrupt priesthood have also come back, over and over again. They were and are also in other lands. Spiritual fascism can arise at any time and in any place. It can play a distorting role in any religion. Political fascism follows or is hand in hand with it, every time.

Happily, in the next life which I shall recount in detail, there was no violent persecution, although the threat of it was certainly a factor. For the first time in many incarnations, I began consciously to return to Goddess worship, though within a Christian context. This was not only an important step for me, but of interest as a real example of how a relationship to the Feminine aspect of divinity can begin to blossom within Christianity. Without persecution, this process could soon mature and bear fruit for many women nowadays. And indeed, there are signs that this is happening. In my past life, I began in irreverence. But what subsequently happened has formed my present life, to a large extent. I was helped in recalling the memory by Jenni Nicholson, a past-life counsellor and therapist who lives in Bath.

8

Rebirth and Wisdom

For me, the more recent past lives are easier to remember. This next life came back with astonishing clarity, once I had started to relax about dates and places.

Account of a Past Life as a Nun and 'Housekeeper'

At the outset of this recall, I found myself standing on a beach and dressed as a nun. Since I knew I had had a life as a nun in Ireland, I then made the mistake of assuming this was an Irish beach. Later, I realized I was in Devon, and this was another incarnation altogether. The time was the late eighteenth to early nineteenth century of the present era.

On my feet I was wearing some bashed-about wooden shoes - though I have no idea if nuns then, or indeed ever, wore such things. Far out in the bay in front of me, I saw a many-sailed ship. It had nothing to do with me or my life and I watched it without curiosity. My real interest lay back at the convent.

Turning back from the beach, I made for my workplace, and was soon taking a detour down a twisting stairway and into a crypt. Father John was there. He had a secret 'still' and was attending to it! This was certainly not any kind of strict establishment, by anyone's rules, though I later found out you could go too far. Father John smiled at me. He was always pleased to see me, for we were in love. I was only twenty years old and he about thirty-five - old enough in my eyes to be romantically mature and very impressive - and we were each other's joy. So far this had only meant an exchange of ideas. And on this day, he took papers from a wooden chest that was kept in the crypt. This was something he wanted to show me, something more secret than the 'still'.

I didn't know why he liked me or wanted to talk to me. He seemed so very much older in every way. There was also a social gulf. He came from a well-to-do family. I was a local girl, a farmer's West Country daughter, with very little education and a wild temperament. My accent was pure Devon and my aspirations were few - in social terms. I also was not interested, at that point, in being a contemplative. What I passionately wanted was passionate life. I was still too young to know what I meant by that. In another century, I might have danced in a nightclub, or run off to join a circus.

Father John was an educated and cultured man. People said he was eccentric but he was popular enough. Everyone seemed to like him. I thought that I fitted in with the side of him that liked the drink and mild rebellion. And yet I knew there was more to it than that. And more to him.

He had a short beard and wore a brownish monk's habit. His eyes were sparkling with enjoyment and dark with wisdom. I looked at him and I thought, 'But you know so much.'

The papers he showed me were someone else's work - an abandoned rough plan for an illuminated manuscript. At least we decided it must have been abandoned. Father John was intrigued. The ideas were heretical. He said that he had met with such concepts before, but never in such developed form. (I don't recall where he got this old manuscript from.) He told me to tell no one about it.

Moving forward in time, I was in bed with Father John. I remember knowing that we were not that worried about being discovered. It was, after all, a very lax establishment. There were rough woollen blankets and no sheets. The stench of these bed-coverings was really quite something! They were hardly ever washed. But what did I care? I was used to it, anyway. And very much in love.

We went on being lovers for quite a while - six months, I

think. He talked to me intensely about ideas he had gathered from the manuscript and from other sources as well. About the marriage of Sun and Moon and about the blessings of the Goddess. Mary the Mother was a Goddess, of equal power with God, though different from Him, in Her ways. This is what he told me. I loved what Father John spoke of. He was disillusioned with orthodox thinking and, as for me, I had never liked it.

We had long talks and he worked out a whole philosophy which he said was much older than Christianity as we knew it. He based it on those papers and his meditations and some hints from strange books he had once read. To me, this was like the door swinging open in an old prison I'd been in so long I couldn't remember when I first had entered it. There was a deep joy in our talks, as in our love-making. We shared joy.

I had read very little, myself - just the Bible and books I was told to read. But I understood all our talks and I loved him very deeply. I loved him for turning my whole world around and showing me the Goddess and teaching me about love and the Great Marriage.

I had not had a desire to be a nun. At the age of sixteen, as a farmer's daughter, I was courted by a fat, elderly aristocrat, an ugly character called Sir Humphrey. I remember my father beseeching me, for the last time, to wed the man - a sixty-year-old lecher with a gross mind in a gross body. My family were not at all well off and they had been bullying me to say yes for some time. My marriage to Sir Humphrey would have been the saving of them. Yet somewhere inside me, I felt it was wrong to couple with a man who only revolted me. I could not explain this to my father - who, anyway, did not want to know. So I quickly invented a religious vocation. We were a Catholic family so they couldn't go against this. But I had never really wanted to be a nun.

In spite of this, I was now very happy. I had my love affair with Father John (and it certainly used to amuse us when he came to hear my confession!). And there was my work, too. I was a 'scribe' and helped to look after the books and manuscripts in the convent. Sometimes, because I was neat and had a good eye for design, I hand-copied prayers and illustrated them. The work was very easy for me, and so I enjoyed it.

Then Father John asked me to meet him one night in an out of the way building, some kind of empty storehouse. He asked me what we were going to do now - about the book and our ideas. Should we hide the new book he had made out of the papers he had found? Or burn it? What should we do? Because, he explained, it could be discovered. All the knowledge was inside us, but should we keep it there and tell no one else? This was a great moral dilemma, he told me. Shouldn't such knowledge be shared? But who, in this place, could we share it with? (Easy going or not, they were not going to congratulate us for heresy!) He asked me what he should do, but really he had made up his own mind. He would go to France. He said that he knew of a secret order there, a Brotherhood he called it, who would take the Book and look after it and make use of the wonderful knowledge and pass it on. In a future time, he said, things might be very different, and the world ready for the knowledge, so it needed to be treasured and carefully preserved so that one day it could be shared with everyone. I said to him, 'all right, we will go.'

Then he told me he was not taking me along. This convent was a much better and safer place for me, he said. He would lose his position in the Church when he left and had terrible, nightmare fears of failing to look after me. This was partly a question of money - he would not have much. But the world out there was no place for a woman without a strong protector, in a strong position. And he just would not be that. I pleaded with him to take me, but he wouldn't change his mind.

Later, he was rowed out into the bay, to a ship that was waiting. He took the Book and he went. It was night and he told no one, except for me. No one saw him go nor suspected anything.

I couldn't believe he had done this. I felt betrayed. What was I to do with the rest of my life, in this (to me, now) meaningless place? If he loved me, I felt, he could not have left me. He would surely have seen that I would rather have died alongside of him! But I was a twenty-year-old girl and he a much older man. Nor did I have any idea, then, of the deep unconscious reasons why he had gone without me.

I became ill for many months. I had a high fever and something wrong with my throat. I spoke of the Book and the ideas we had shared. As I began to recover, I often found Mother Superior and other nuns and also some priests gathered round my bed. They were asking me questions. I did not tell them where Father John had gone. Except in the vaguest terms, I did not know. He was safe from them, therefore. Soon, they decided it was all Father John's fault - that he had corrupted me. I was to be watched carefully, at least for a while, and re-educated in the true faith. They put me in a blue robe, to convalesce, and filled my room with flowers.

I still did not know what to do with my life. I hated the place and all the people in it. They were not cruel and yet struck me as all pinched up and withered. Mother Superior's face looked like a dead candle! Some of the others, I told myself, had skin like pig lard! Their spirits were small, how could they stand it? Their lives were mean. So I went on, in my young grief and frustration.

Then I turned to the Lady Mary for help. I prayed to Her as Goddess to show me what to do next. She gave me an astonishing vision of how life could change, for everyone. How everything could be different for women. I saw them being educated as highly as men were and living lives of such freedom that I had not dreamed of and dressing like boys and riding horseback - astride! And marrying or not, according to their *own* choice. And I saw that the Goddess was beginning to be worshipped again.

One day, whispered Mother Mary, one day.

I saw women giving the laying-on-of-hands and all kinds of other healing that looked to be mystical. But no one did that! No woman could heal except by ordinary everyday herbal potions, to nurse family or friends. Well, there were old women in the villages, sometimes, whose healing was on a more mysterious level, but they were at risk of being accused of witchcraft.

Yes, but I knew I could do it! And I saw clearly a world where women healed and taught. And another thing! I would write my own beliefs down, if I lived in that future. I wanted to write down my *own* words. Why should I always be copying out the things that men said? I wanted *my* words to be written, and not to have them dismissed as the scribblings of a mere woman!

(And in this world of the future, I could have gone away with Father John. He would have taken me with him. I believed that, strongly.)

This was the vision that Mary gave to me.

I began to do a lot of things on my own that felt like spells - though I did not have any idea why I knew how to do them. It just seemed to start happening, when I felt strongly. One day, when the chapel was empty, I climbed into the pulpit and I made an invocation. I said that in time to come, *women* would preach in all churches, as often as men. But the things that they preached about would be very different from what was said now. They would tell of the Sun and Moon and about Mary the Goddess, as well as God the Father. They would explain about everyone's soul having freedom to learn and grow in its own way. And there would be no more evil nonsense about burning in hell fires for ever if your ideas were different from the priests'.

Another day, I was standing before the altar and She gave me a vision of a white dove. She said, 'I am the Holy Spirit. I give life. I am love.' And a rain of silver light fell over me. But when I asked what more I could do with my life now, She only showed me an apple tree.

I did a lot more spells and invocations for the worship of the Goddess to be on Earth. And I offered myself at the altar, with a solemn vow that in some future life I should work as Her priestess. I believed that we have a great many lives, for Father John had told me of it. Besides, I had begun to feel I could remember some other ones.

Then one day, at twilight, I was working magic at the altar. I had some things laid out upon it, stones and other bits I had found on the beach nearby. Mother Superior came in and caught me. She swept the things off the altar and talked to me about evil and 'devil's work'. I would not get away with it this time, she said.

Later, I was interviewed by two priests. I expected to be treated harshly but I couldn't have cared less. I felt there was not much left for me to hope for in this life. Then the younger one, Father Benedict, made a sideways joke about letting me off if I became his mistress. It was all done with a nod and a wink and an implication that this was *only* a joke, though in bad taste, when you think of it. But we all knew it was serious. The older priest looked shocked, but he could do nothing. Father Benedict was from a wealthy family, who contributed greatly to Church funds. You just did not annoy people like that!

Later on, when we were alone, I gave him my answer. I would become his housekeeper - officially - and whore - unofficially. Well, why not, I thought? I took it as a kindly deed on his part, though the self-interest was obvious. He did not believe in execution of witches (They had stopped hanging them, in these days, but still you didn't know just what would be done to you.) He was very much against what he saw as ignorant persecution. He told me it was time for reason to prevail. My actions he took for a superstitious foible. Father Benedict was a worldly man, though he had a kind heart, a Churchman who knew on which side his bread was buttered and would always make sure he got what he wanted, though without any viciousness or subterfuge. His was not an enquiring mind. We did not share ideas, but he was gentle and considerate in bed. Tall, slim and dark-haired, with an astute face, he was not at all bad looking. I could not say I loved him in any way, but I *liked* him well enough and was grateful to him.

Father Benedict was active in parish business and with Church politics. He was very often out. I had nothing to do really, all day. 'Housekeeper' was a name, not much more than that. There were other servants for the chores and the cook knew how to run things. I wore pretty dresses and walked in the garden. My vows as a nun had, of course, been absolved, though Father Benedict had persuaded everyone, 'for the good name of the convent and reputations of the local priests', to hush up the real reasons. I had little tasks to do in the house, and that was all. No friends came to visit me. I had lost touch with the other farmers' daughters I had grown up with. Besides, my social status was now too - unclear? My family felt the shame deeply and more or less abandoned me. Twice, I had given them cause to feel upset. They let me know that the first time, they had not felt justified in saying a word about it. But all was different now! The life I led made a mockery of my

early vocation! And a mockery, therefore, of their own sacri-
fice, in losing the financial assistance of Sir Humphrey, on the
altar of the local convent.

Sometimes, out of sheer boredom and loneliness, I helped
Cook to get the dinner, even though I need not have done.
She was grateful, she said, for the kind thought, though not for
my cack-handed cooking skills! I thought she just let me be
with her because she took pity on me.

The books that Father Benedict had were not inspiring at all.
I did not like to read them. But eventually I saw that, with all
this free time, I could be writing down my own words in this
very life. I did not ever conceive a child. I did not know why
this was but was very glad of it. I had plenty of time and could
be writing things. No one would ever read them but that
wouldn't matter. I'd do it for myself and for Mother Mary.

It was a problem that I had no paper or pens of my own. But
if I did for Father Benedict the things that he wanted in bed, I
knew he'd give them to me. And he did, very easily, as often as
I wanted. What are you doing? he asked. Are you keeping a
diary? He felt that it was a most suitable thing for a woman to
be doing and I began to worry in case he asked to see it. But he
was not really that interested. He just liked being generous and
giving me what I wanted. He felt that we both had a most
'suitable arrangement'.

I wrote and wrote. My ideas about religion, love poems for
Father John, hymns to the Goddess Mary. I also wrote what I
thought of as spells to get Father John to come back. One day,
I thought, I will see him again. If not in this life, it will be in
another one. But let it be in this life! (Though I did not really
believe that it would be.) I buried some copies of these in the
garden, to make the magic more powerful. And I did other
spells with flowers and my own spoken words. More spells for
Father John's safety and for our reunion. The Cook helped me
to do this, though she didn't know she did. She talked to me
about a fortune teller she had once known very well, and who
taught her some love spells. I picked up tips from her. Just very
simple things, folk-lorish, really. But I knew how to use them.

Years passed, then Father Benedict died. I was not that
young, I thought, though I had not kept count of the time pass-

ing. I didn't know if he had made any provision for me, but if he had, I didn't get it. His successor threw me out.

I did not think I would find a new protector now. And I was right. Soon, I died in a poorhouse, of a recurrence of the fever I had when Father John left. My book remained in the house. I don't know what happened to it. All I knew was he had not come back.

* * * * *

I realized during this recall that Father John was the man I now know as J., the same priest with whom I had been executed in Atlantis very long ago. In the light of this, his decision to leave me behind looks as though it could have had more profound motivation than merely that of a man abandoning his mistress, on the grounds 'he travels fastest who travels alone'. Other than this, what strikes me as powerful and moving is the idea of a nun, a country girl in early nineteenth-century Devon, having such strong convictions about women's freedom and their potential and the great difference it would make if a feminine Deity were acknowledged, not just in the ordinary candle-lighting and 'Hail Mary' way, but really as a Goddess. (Her easiness with witchcraft is quite a surprise, too. The Witchcraft Act of 1735 had made the official execution of witches illegal. But, unofficially, there could still be violence, meted out by fanatical people with a personal interest, as she must have known. And within the Church, the practice of even a positive and healing witchcraft was still regarded with suspicion, as it is to this day. As for Her Pagan worship of Mary as a Deity, she must have been perfectly aware of how this would be perceived, both within the Church and in the community at large.)

However, this was a time of pioneering feminist thinkers and - by what? synchronicity? - an uneducated young woman began to have related thoughts, under the stimulus of heretical teachings and along rather more mystical than social lines. She did not feel it necessary to abandon the spiritual, in order that women should have more freedom, but to transform our concepts of what the spiritual is. And in taking this line, she

moved towards a feeling of spiritual solidarity with women. Or
at least, she envisaged that. I imagine there must have been
many others like her. Free-spirited but lonely. Unknown
visionaries, unable to share what they saw or explain its implications. And more devoted to it than to the great issues of the
time, to which she seems to have paid very little attention (the
Napoleonic wars, the Battle of Trafalgar, etc.) But what, now
seems more important - to a woman of our own time? Old
European wars or early feminism?

Direct Revelation

To continue my own story, right into the present life - in
August 1978, I became a self-initiated witch on the path of solitary wisewoman, a logical outcome of experiments with nature
magic in that former life which I have just described, and a def-
inite re-affirmation of my return to the worship of the Goddess.
I found in the last vestiges of our native tradition the religious
and magical practices I had been looking for. It also seems to
me that this initiation was a regaining of the spiritual perspective which I had once discovered in neolithic Britain, in my life
then at Avebury and also in the Chilterns. Since no one can
turn the clock right back to a former age, this present day
embracing of the wisewoman role was not a literal return to the
Old Faith, as it once was practised, but a reinterpretation of
oneness with nature, in a style appropriate for now.

Becoming a witch has remained both a healing and empow-
ering experience and is also important to me because of feminist implications. Society has defined the woman spell-caster
as evil (far more so than her male counterpart, though he, too,
has suffered persecution). What I mean by 'witchcraft' is the
working of word-magic, through charms and incantations,
within the context of reverence for the spirit manifested in
nature, for the purpose of helping to restore health and happiness. A mystical and 'natural' healer or local enchantress. It's a
very long way from the stereotypical wart-covered 'hexer', who,
if she ever really existed, was a rare and unhappy soul, outnum-
bered by her wisewoman sisters.

In August 1991 I became also a priestess of Mari, in the Fellowship of Isis, ordained by Olivia Robertson, through telepathic attunement and in private ritual. Thus, I resumed a ministry started long ago in Atlantis. This closed a cycle of incarnations, spanning many thousands of years, and opened a new cycle. Or spiral, perhaps.

This year, I was told clearly by my inner guide that I have always worshipped the Goddess Mari, no matter what religion I have formally accepted. I have been Her priestess in the Sea temples of Atlantis and worshipped Her as Mary in Christianity and served Her as Goddess of the Moon and as the Lady Marian in modern witchcraft. This is the name by which I have most often called upon the Dark Goddess. However, She has many names and is beyond every one of them. She is the Deep Feminine Power who rules the inner tides as well as the oceans. The great sea of the realm of dreams and psychic perception is Hers, as is the womb. She is the darkness that transforms us and gives birth to the light. The ebb and flow of destiny is also Hers, for She not only grants us psychic perception - whatever our spiritual tradition - but rules all the laws of psychic connection, all the unseen influences and the links that outlast death.

She is always of the subtle, mysterious and magical, and we find Her in our sexual passion or in death or birth, for in these - as well as in deep meditation or the spontaneous effect upon the soul of a sudden distress or joy - the doors of psychic perception can be flung wide open.

Invocations of Her, by whatever name we call Her, can bring a purification, a strong purgation, as in the action of a fever clearing toxins from the body, preceding a gradual resurgence of good health, but on any level of our being and in any dimension. She is not 'only' the coolness and silence of night but also, since Her nature includes its own opposite, the great healing power of heat and catharsis. She is both wise and loving, yet never a soft option.

The teachings which I have received in life after life, and from the Inner Realms, state that She and the Bright God in Darkness, by whatever name we know Him, are at one, in love. And the aim of the current return of the worship of the

Goddess is to rebalance both the male and female and inaugurate an age when deity is worshipped in aspects both Feminine and Masculine. For now, there should be an emphasis on the Feminine, to offset many thousands of years of violent patriarchy, the long, sad history of the persecution of all women who attempted to live as wisewomen or priestesses and the terrible social, political and sexual oppression all over the world - crimes of sexual violence, clitoridectomies, forced child-bearing, limiting of opportunities. But when the true nature of the Feminine is found and worshipped, the true nature of the Masculine (something as unlike patriarchy as freedom is unlike prison or love unlike hate) begins to surface at the same time. This new spiritual Way, for both sexes, non-dogmatic and gentle, shall help to heal all our relationships with one another and with the Earth. And the key to it all is in the hands, not of the Bright Goddess of Physical Abundance and Manifest Beauty, but of the Dark Goddess of the Soul and the Mysteries.

I have said that the Dark Goddess can only be honoured by an acceptance of the personal in our lives, whether man or woman. The equation of feminine with personal and the subsequent disparagement of both has meant a denial of the blessings of the Dark Goddess by one and all. Perhaps it was necessary to turn away from Her, in order to fully develop an *awareness* of ourselves as separate entities, distinct from other life forms and from one another. Perhaps the alienation and loneliness of the isolated ego is somehow a necessary stage on the long road to complete wisdom. And certainly a strong development of human objectivity has allowed intellectual activities and some forms of research to flourish and blossom, together with a particular kind of psychological stance, a detachment from ones own needs, which can actually overcome selfishness. But it is now vital to recognize once again the value of personal, subjective experience. For it is our only real access to the spiritual (which, without personal experience, remains just theory). The Dark Goddess's touch is felt in the intimate areas of our lives, where most women are at ease - as are confident men. The places where we are born or conceive, give birth and dream, say our most private and heartfelt prayers and help others through their death - or die ourselves. These are all realms which our culture has stripped of most inner meaning and much dignity. Daring to prize and to share our spiritual-sensory experience and private spiritual understanding is the only way to begin to reconsecrate human life. This far transcends any narrow definition of religious tradition. (I have seen it practised by people of many different beliefs.)

That we do not now find this easy is hardly a surprise. Personal psychic experience and direct revelation has been regarded as potential heresy, in Europe and in other parts of the world, too. One reason for this, in the past, was that it questioned the authority of the Catholic church. It still does. In fact it questions the attitude that any holy man (or woman) can get it right for the rest of us, and that his or her revelations are true and 'objective' while ours are false, subjective and dangerous. An institution that wanted spiritual dominance, complete enough to affect all secular activities as well as private life, must have found it very useful to be able to say, 'Your spiritual communications and visions, however seemingly reasonable and enlightened, are really demonic.' (Imagine being able to say this to anyone who disagreed with you!) 'The spirit messages you say you receive are actually evil. That's because of who you are. Or rather, who you are not! If you won't stop talking about them, I have *carte blanche* to persecute you or even execute you.'

The same prohibition exists nowadays, but in more subtle forms and not only from the Church. Big Brother still feels free to attack any signs of spiritual autonomy, in case it should undermine the present power structures or challenge his own ideas on distribution of wealth in relation to a person's supposed worthiness to receive. The difference is, there is less collective acceptance of his *religious* decrees.

Taking back the authority of direct revelation is a subversive act. It is based on understanding that there is no entirely objective rendering of the spiritual and that a subjective perception has is own validity. There is really only a consensus (sometimes voluntary and sometimes imposed) of personal beliefs aligned with the transpersonal.

We must reject the idea that direct revelation is spurious or irrelevant, because it's all we have on which to base any real *feeling* for sanctity. And it is only in our personal experience in prayer or meditation or any spontaneous psychic experience, or revelation through art, or within the Mysteries of Love, Birth or Death, that we each, paradoxically, transcend isolation. As the novelist and diarist Anais Nin once commented, 'if you go deeply enough, the personal life really goes beyond [its limitations] and reaches universality.'

The methods I have used to explore my own spiritual orientation and to develop a personal sense of understanding and inner vision have been described in this book. I recommend them to you, reader, whoever you are. They may not lead you to the same conclusions or experiences as my own, for though truth is constant it has many facets. But we all live our many lives in relationship with the Dark Goddess, whether consciously or not and whether of any kind of priesthood or of the laity. And though it may be that your own inclination is to worship primarily a Bright Goddess of the manifest world, yet She is the sister to the Dark Goddess and is Her other Self.

There are no final words to summarize the Dark Goddess's attributes. By definition, She is the Mystery. Apart from the cries and sighs of sexual passion or the sounds made in extremis or in joyful birth, only a line from a poem can invoke Her. Or a few lines meant as poetry. So here are mine.

It takes a long time for all souls to grow wings. As long as it takes for a crystal egg to hatch out as a bird made of flesh and blood. But the Goddess works miracles. She has all time. The crystal egg will hatch out by the Moon's cool light and the bird grow from fledgeling to a free-flyer, though its home is here on the Earth. It *is* Earth on the wing. (A metaphor for ecstatic being, the deep sense of communion with all life.) This is foretold by Her for every creature. The crystal egg and the bird. She has dreamt them, at Dark Moon.

Appendix A

For people who want to learn about Goddess worship in the present day, the Fellowship of Isis is an international organiztion that might be of interest. Membership is free and open to all, regardless of race, gender, or religious affiliations. Isis is the Goddess of "ten thousand names," and the Fellowship acknowledges Her as the beauty and truth of Rhiannon, Tara, Aphrodite, Demeter, Persephone, Iamanja - or the Virgin Mary, to name a few. Members are encouraged to find their own spiritual direction, to worship any Goddess or God of their choosing. Emphasis, as appropriate for this time, is on Goddess mysteries, yet the importance of polarity is stressed. The principles upheld by the Fellowship as a whole are Love, Beauty and Truth. Rites can be studied and performed by friends and families. These rites consist mainly of spoken invocations and offerings (for example, of flowers or incense), followed by a meditation and channeling of healing. They are easily adaptable for solitary worshippers. Ordained priestesses or priests are also welcome and encouraged to join.

Write to: Olivia Robertson
             The Fellowship of Isis
             Clonegal Castle
             Clonegal, Enniscorthy
             Wexford
             Ireland

Appendix B

The following are some prayers, given by my inner guide, to the Dark Goddess and the God who partners Her.

>Dark Mother of All Life
>Great Goddess of the Tides
>from your eternal womb, that deep inner sea,
>may each human soul be reborn in harmony.
>So may we live with one another
>and with all Earth's creatures,
>in wisdom and health.
>Take from us our cruelty and falsehood.
>Let these ebb and die.
>Let flow in us love and truth.

•   •   •

>Bright Lord in the Darkness,
>All Father, we call on you
>to quicken all our dreams
>of the harmony and beauty
>of Earth restored.
>Make fertile all our visions
>of the peace that could be,
>and of the Earth again radiant and unspoiled.
>Healer and guardian, by your law of love,
>So may this be.

Bibliography

Anderson, Flavia, *The Ancient Secret* (Research into Lost Knowledge Organisation, 1988)

Ashcroft-Nowicki, Dolores, *The New Book of the Dead* (Aquarian/Thorsons, 1992)

Begg, Ean, *The Cult of the Black Virgin* (Arkana, 1985)

Berlitz, Charles, *Atlantis* (Macmillan, 1984)

Beth, Rae, *Hedge Witch: A Guide to Solitary Witchcraft* (Robert Hale, 1990)

Brennan, J.H., *The Reincarnation Workbook* (Aquarian Press, 1984)

Crowley, Vivianne, *Wicca: The Old Religion in the New Age* (Aquarian Press, 1989)

Drury, Nevill, *The Gods of Rebirth* (Prism Press, 1988)

Durdin-Robertson, Lawrence, *God the Mother: Creatress and Giver of Life* (Cesara Publications, 1989)

— *Life in the Next World* (Cesara Publications)

Farrant, Sheila, *Symbols for Women: A Matrilineal Zodiac* (Unwin Paperbacks, 1989)

Fortune, Dion, *Moon Magic* (Samuel Weiser, 1978)

— *The Sea Priestess* (Aquarian Press, 1989)

Glaskin, G.M., *Windows of the Mind* (Arrow Books, 1974)

Green Marian, *The Elements of Natural Magic* (Element Books, 1989)

Guirdham, Arthur, *The Cathars and Reincarnation* (C.W. Daniel, 1990)

Hope, Murry, *Practical Atlantean Magic* (Aquarian Press, 1991)

Matthews, Caitlin, *Arthur and the Sovereignty of Britain - King and Goddess in the Mabinogion* (Arkana, 1989)

— *Sophia, Goddess of Wisdom* (Aquarian Press, 1991)

—*The Elements of the Goddess* (Element Books, 1989)

Matthews, Caitlin and John, *Ladies of the Lake* (Aquarian Press, 1992)

Matthews, John, and Green, Marian, *The Grail Seeker's Companion - A guide to the Grail Quest in the Aquarian Age* (Aquarian Press, 1986)

McVickar Edwards, Carolyn, *The Storyteller's Goddess - Tales of the Goddess and Her Wisdom from Around the World* (Harper, San Francisco, 1991)

Nin, Anais, *A Woman Speaks* (W.H.Allen, 1978)

Noble, Vicki, *Shakti Woman - Feeling our Fire, Healing our World* (Harper, San Francisco, 1991)

Raine, Kathleen, *Defending Ancient Springs* (Golgonooza Press, 1985)

Redgrove, Peter, *The Black Goddess and the Sixth Sense* (Paladin Books, 1989)

Richardson, Alan, *Earth God Rising - The Return of the Male Mysteries* (Llewellyn Publications, 1990)

Robertson, Olivia, *Dea - Rites and Mysteries of the Goddess* (Cesara Publications, 1988)

— *Maya - Goddess Rites for Solo Use* (Cesara Publications, 1992)

— *Ordination of Priestesses and Priests* (Cesara Publications, 1983)

— *Sophia - Cosmic Consciousness of the Goddess* (Cesera Publications, 1986)

— *Urania - Ceremonial Magic of the Goddess* (Cesera Publications, 1983)

Sjoo, Monica and Mor, Barbara, *The Great Cosmic Mother - Rediscovering the Religion of Earth* (Harper and Row, 1987)

Starhawk, *Truth or Dare - Encounters with Power, Authority and Mystery* (Harper and Row, San Francisco, 1987)

Stewart, R.J., *Earth Light - Rediscovering the Wisdom of Celtic and Faery Lore* (Element Books, 1992)

TenDam, Hans, *Exploring Reincarnation* (Arkana, 1990)

Travers, P.L., *What the Bee Knows* (Aquarian Press, 1989)

Walker, Barbara G., *The Crone - Women of Age, Wisdom and Power* (Harper, San Francisco, 1985)

— *The Woman's Encyclopedia of Myths and Secrets* (Harper and Row, San Francisco, 1983)

Whitton, Joel L., and Fisher, Joe, *Life Between Life* (Grafton Books, 1986)

Zink, Dr David, *The Stones of Atlantis* (W.H. Allen, 1978)